SHINE

SHINE

An Entrepreneur's Journey for Building a
Highly Successful Business and a Healthy Life

ADAM ZBAR

CEO of Sun Basket, the Healthy Eating Company

**FOREWORD BY
TYLER MACNIVEN**

TYCHO
PRESS

Interior Designer: Michael Cook
Cover Designer: Kristine Brogno
Art Manager: Amy Burditt
Editor: Lia Brown
Production Editor: Erum Khan

ISBN: Print 978-1-64152-647-0 | eBook 978-1-64152-648-7

Contents

Foreword

It was pre-dawn; nearly freezing in the Marin Headlands. However, the cold did not phase Adam. He was pumping with excitement as he embarked upon the two-mile upward trail. The path itself starts flat, slowly slopes, and then takes a turn, then starts to ascend. A calming energy enveloped us as a silky mist hovered quietly in the valley. This should be a friendly morning jog between friends, yet I know Adam really wanted to beat me to the top.

"Tell me more about your relationship with your father?" he asks.

Is he actually curious? Or is he trying to tire my breath?

"I love the man. He taught me to save my words for the top." I smile and push past him.

We call this Heartbreak Hill, because after over a mile of running uphill, the second half becomes offensively steep. It is the kind of steep that will slide your feet back down if you don't get a good purchase with each step. The kind of steep that gets you panting so hard, your lungs burn for days.

There is no more banter now. I'm using every ounce of power to dig my legs up the hill. I am ten years younger than Adam, and I am in better shape. I should beat him. I feel my thighs start to grow heavy and slow. I hear him panting behind me. He's close. He's next to me. He's barely ahead of me. Head down. I know his tactic. He focuses in on a rock, a stick, or a plant a few feet ahead then runs to it. Then he picks a new target and runs to that. My eyes are blurry and can't focus. I try to reach out and yank him back by his sweater. My fingers brush the fabric but can't get a grip. He is just beyond reach. Ten steps ahead. Fifteen. I feel the precise moment my will breaks. Snap. I slow to a desperate panting walk. Adam continues to steam up the hill.

I round the final bend at the top. Adam is waiting for me, his breath nearly restored. He releases a mighty howl. Moments later the sun breaks over the horizon and fills the bay with such loving morning light. The sunrise is our gold medal for getting up early and making it all the way up. We hoot and holler together, celebrating the arrival of another exciting day. We are being supercharged by the sun.

"How can we take the energy we felt on the mountain this morning and share it with all our customers?" Adams asks me at a coffee shop an hour later. We had begun our weekly "Sun Runs" a few months earlier, right around the same time we decided to explore the idea of starting a healthy meal kit company. The idea was to utilize a meal kit business model to make it easier for people around the country eat healthy and delicious meals.

"We should definitely have the word 'sun' in the name," we agree.

"Sun Farms?"

"Sunny Box?"

"Sun Box!" That's it! That's it. That's it?

I leave the coffee shop, and when I get home, I see Adam has texted two words. "Sun Basket."

Much better. I absolutely love the name Sun Basket. It symbolizes life. Energy. The positivity around healthy eating.

"Oh yes. That is it," I reply.

The company that started with four of us in my living room is now a 1,700-person operation that ships millions of healthy meals a month to folks in all of the lower forty-eight states. Holy cow, is this some sort of psychedelic dream?! How on earth did this happen?

I can say without a doubt that none of it would have gotten off the ground without Adam's superhuman drive and leadership. The same power he used to beat me up the hill in the morning was brought into every aspect of the company's development.

There is a must-see video of a bearded, philosophical Steve Jobs saying, "The minute that you understand that you can poke life and actually something will pop out the other side, that you can change it, that you can mold it. That's maybe the most important thing."

Adam pokes at life. He pokes at it big-time. He wakes up before the sun and starts poking. He does it because he knows that he can make a positive impact on the world and for his family. His secret to success is his continuous focus, discipline, and hard work. The more he pokes at life, the more it pokes back, and that energizes him. Adam has more energy circling inside him than almost anyone I have ever met. He is either 100 percent completely on and functioning, or asleep. He's like a laptop that still works at maximum efficiency even at 1 percent charge, but only when it hits 0 percent will it turn off. He can be writing a sentence on his computer, fall asleep for several hours, then wake up and finish the sentence as if the nap never happened.

When Adam approaches a problem, he paces around it, inspecting all sides, like a lion stalking its prey. His eyes lock onto it with laser focus. He asks the people next to him what they think. He'll rephrase his questions and ask them again. He'll listen to the data. He does everything in his power to understand the problem fully before leaping on top of it, wrestling it to the ground, and completely solving it. He'll wrap it in a bow, stand up, brush himself off, and look for the next one.

However, when I met Adam thirteen years ago, he was a lot less balanced. He was 50 pounds heavier, and his work life seemed to control him in an unhealthy way. As you read his book you'll learn why he needed to go to a darker, unhealthy place to realize the key to regaining control over his destiny would come from within.

My friendship with Adam is a friendship of encouragement, intense (but very friendly) competition, and support. In the last five years, we have both gotten engaged, married, and had children. We achieved our goal of starting a company that empowers people all over the country to live healthier lives. We produced a feature film, which recently got accepted into the SF Indie Film Festival. We have brainstormed hundreds of ideas and run up many mountains. We've discussed the importance of nurturing the self, our families, our friends, and larger communities. We have asked each other big life questions and contemplated the universe. We have pushed each other into freezing winter lakes. We have kept each other guessing. I am incredibly lucky to be his friend. I have learned so much about what is possible from Adam.

As you read his story, I hope you'll find the same encouragement and inspiration that I have felt being his friend and co-founder. The lessons in this book will have you run faster up that hill, launch that start-up that's always been in the back of your mind, or just be a better partner, sibling, or friend. Soak in all the sunshine that radiates from his words and stories.

—Tyler MacNiven
The Amazing Race Winner, Co-Founder Sunbasket.com

CHAPTER 1

Red Alert: Mission Control, We Have a Problem

"Things don't look good."

I sat in the doctor's office, waiting for him to return. It was the first time that I'd been to a doctor in over ten years, despite my father, who's a scientist, telling me that I needed to go. I'd finally selected a doctor after asking a friend for a recommendation. The doctor he'd recommended was frankly a bit strange. He brought both his dogs into the office, and he seemed really depressed. He had good reason because his wife had recently died from terminal cancer. I couldn't even imagine what that would be like. While I felt for him, it still made me feel uncomfortable that he looked disheveled and seemed distracted. As I sat there waiting for him to come back, I thought about leaving. I didn't like that he seemed to have trouble reading the results from my blood work and that he sneezed a few times while reading the charts and had wiped his nose with the back of his sleeve. I also didn't like that he took forever to say anything before he said simply, "Things don't look good," and then promptly left the room before I could ask him what that meant.

The past four years had been rough. I was thirty-nine years old and to my calculation 50 pounds overweight. Those pounds hadn't come on all at once. Rather, they had come on over the four years of running my venture capital–backed start-up Zannel (which in hindsight was a terrible name, by the way—but more on that later . . .). I'd won a Webby for Best Mobile Social Network, added three million users to the platform, and had beamed with pride when either TechCrunch or Mashable, I can't remember which one, wrote an article saying that if Facebook and Twitter had a baby it would be Zannel. We had the most sophisticated video, picture, and text sharing across mobile and web in 2005. You read that right—years before Instagram made this behavior ubiquitous. We'd also raised money from top-tier venture capitalists on Sand Hill Road. I'd raised $16 million to date and had followed my dream to become a tech entrepreneur. That was the good news. The bad news was that the stress level had been way higher than I'd ever expected—I hadn't slept through the night in six months, I'd gained weight, and I was in the middle of a divorce. In hindsight, given where I am today, only one word describes where I was then: yikes!

The doctor came back into the room, adjusted his greasy glasses, and patted his golden retriever—who also needed a bath—on the head. The dog lazily looked up at the doctor, then back over to me, and then back down. The dullness in the dog's eyes depressed me. So did the fact that the doctor still hadn't said anything since he'd returned to the room. So what was it? Did I have some sort of disease? I'd always been terrified that I would get cancer ever since I was a little kid. My father, Dr. Bert Zbar, has been a leading cancer researcher at the National Institutes of Health for over forty years. During that time, he discovered four of the first twenty genes that cause hereditary kidney cancer. As an entrepreneur who felt like I was on the precipice of failing right before turning forty and who was clearly in poor health, my dad's shoes seemed impossibly large to fill.

I'd grown up with my father telling me about all the things that cause cancer. Spend too much time out in the sun and, son, you'll get cancer. Better to lather yourself with sunblock and try to stay out of the sun. My favorite food as a kid—hot dogs— also was off the list because they contained sodium nitrate, which my father had said caused cancer. Barbecuing meat, according to my father, also increased your risk of cancer. My father explained to me that cancer was the mutation of your cells, which turned into a tumor. It seemed like there were so many ways your cells could mutate that I'd grown up terrified that I was going to get cancer. Colon cancer. Stomach cancer. Esophagus cancer. I wasn't sure what was going to go wrong. However, a large part of the reason I hadn't gone to the doctor in the past decade was that I was terrified that the moment I walked into the doctor's office, he would tell me that I had cancer. And now here I was in this absent-minded doctor's office, and all he had said to me so far was, "Things don't look good." It was enough to make someone who normally didn't have hypochondriac tendencies start going into worrying overdrive.

"Doc. Doc, are you okay?" I said after the doctor looked down wearily, seemed poised to cry, and slumped down next to me in the seat next to his dog. He turned away for a moment, wiped a tear from his eye and told me that in truth he wasn't doing so well.

His wife had fought a long, hard struggle against cancer. He had been at her bedside when she passed away recently. I thought that it must have been even harder being a doctor and knowing that there was nothing he could do to help his wife fix herself. He said that he brought his dogs into the office because they made him feel less lonely and because she had loved them so much. They reminded him of her. In my mind, it was clear that this doctor should have taken a sabbatical or at least some time off after his wife passed away. However, because we had just met, I didn't feel like it was my right to tell him anything about how he should lead his life. I did want to know, however, what he had meant when he said that "things don't look good."

The doctor looked up from his charts over his half-rim glasses and stared at me for a long moment. He asked a simple question, "Do you eat breakfast?" This had been a sore subject between my father and me for the past twenty-plus years. My dad believed, like any good doctor, that filling your body with nutrients and fuel in the morning was good for you. It curbed your hunger later in the day and it gave you more consistent energy. However, I had never done it because, in my mind, given that I was now overweight, skipping breakfast meant that I ate fewer calories. Fewer calories resulted in the potential for weight loss. It was a simple equation. How many calories came in versus the number of calories burned. The fallacy, I would later learn, was twofold. Number one was that by skipping breakfast, I became so hungry by lunch and dinner that I didn't think about what I was putting into my body and I ate too much. The second problem was the quality of what I was putting into my body was loaded with processed carbohydrates, which spiked my glycemic load and led my body to store fat versus processing the sugar-rich foods. The result?—I was now 50 pounds overweight.

Another part of the problem was that I'd always been an athlete. I'd grown up skiing, hiking, running, surfing, and playing sports all through high school. That seemed like a good thing, no? Well, of course exercise is great for your body. However, for me, like I learned about a lot of weekend warrior athletes, I used exercise as a crutch to justify whatever I was putting into my body. Three slices of pizza and five martinis on a Friday night? No problem, since I got up early on Saturday mornings and ran five miles to the Golden Gate Bridge and back. Burgers, French fries, and a Coke for lunch? No problem. I was bonding with the engineers on my team who loved to down burgers and fries with endless rounds of sugary soft drinks. Compared to these guys, I was super healthy, I'd thought, since before work I'd go for thirty-minute runs. The problem was that my body hadn't kept up with this endless assault from my poor diet. The pizza, martinis, burgers, fries, burritos, nachos, etc. had taken a toll on my body that my level of exercise couldn't compensate for.

This pattern started when I was in high school and I switched from playing soccer to football. Football was the most popular sport in Salt Lake City, where I grew up, and I imagined myself under the Friday night lights, streaking down the sideline, catching a tightly thrown spiral, and running into the end zone to the screaming excitement of the packed stands. It was simple. I was smitten by girls and thought that football was the sport that would most impress them.

I was younger than most of the other guys on the team because my birthday was in October. I was also really skinny at sixteen years old because I'd grown something like eight inches between my sophomore and junior years. The coach had asked me to switch positions to outside linebacker given my new height and told me to "hit the weights to put on some muscle."

Looking now at the huge professional football players who distort their bodies with oversized muscles, which often cause them health issues as they get older and the muscle turns to fat, I cringe. However, at the time, the idea that I could spend all summer in the weight room lifting weights with the coolest kids in school sounded awesome. I always was a goal-driven kid, so I set my first ambitious goal—I was going to be able to bench press 225 pounds, since that was what I saw the senior football players doing. That weight, 225 pounds, is basically a 45-pound bar plus four weights, two on each side of the bar, weighing 45 pounds each. Every day I worked out at the gym with my friend Tom as my spotter. Tom and I had grown up together, and he had always towered over me because he was both a year older and by natural body type a hulking man. Tom played nose guard for Olympus High School, where we both went, following in the footsteps of his brother Art who had played the same position. I was his scrawny, brainy friend who was always playing jokes on him, racing around on my bike, and telling him about what I wanted to do when I grew up. I wanted to be an entrepreneur like my grandfather, George Hatch, who had founded some of Salt Lake City's major TV and radio stations and ran one of Utah's oldest newspapers. My grandfather drove a Jeep, loved ice cream, and was a brilliant man. I was going to be an entrepreneur like him, but instead I was going to live in

Hawaii since I loved everything about the island lifestyle. But more on that later . . .

Each day after practice, Tom and I would come home exhausted. We'd always head to his house because it was closer to school. Also because his mom stocked the fridge with just what Tom and I thought we needed for our bodies—tons of calories. The normal day featured Tom and I taking off our pads and then having a milk-chugging contest. Each of us would try to down a gallon of milk before the other one finished. In hindsight, I'm surprised that his mother didn't get upset that we were drinking all their milk every day and drinking straight from the jug. However, as a sixteen-year-old fast-growing boy who wanted to put on lots of muscle and strengthen my bones, drinking as much milk as possible seemed like a healthy thing to do. From there, the next thing that Tom and I loved to do was microwave a bunch of frozen burritos. We'd eat multiple at a time. During two-a-days, when we had two football practices in the span of one day, we would also order an extra-large pizza with pepperoni on it. While pepperoni, like hot dogs, had sodium nitrate in it, I was so over the moon about its flavor that I went against my dad's edict about processed meats and ordered it anyway.

All the carb loading and heavy-weight lifting worked, and over the course of two years I added more than 50 pounds to my lanky frame. I loved to take pictures with my girlfriend, Marni, with my shirt off, especially at the local water park. I was tan, buffed, and thought that I looked really cool. Everything was working out for me, too, I thought. I was a straight-A student; I was on the journalism team as the assistant school paper editor; I had a cool, beautiful girlfriend; and I was a decent football player. While I wasn't nearly as good as the guys who had grown up playing football since they were ten years old, I was pretty good. The coach made me a strong side outside linebacker, and I loved the role because it allowed me to go after the quarterback and try to tackle him. It was a very simple goal I could get my head around. As I went from 150 pounds to over 200 pounds of buffed muscle, I reached my goal of benching 225 pounds and then exceeded it. At my strongest point, I started benching 360 pounds in sets, something that I would have never thought possible when the first time I benched with Tom, I could barely bench the 45-pound bar plus a dime, 10 pounds, on each side.

I left high school on a high and went to a small liberal arts college called Pomona College. It was the same school that my grandfather had gone to, and as I idolized his entrepreneurial career, I thought going there would be good for me, too. In actuality, it was a terrific school that focused on teaching students in small class sizes on a beautiful campus at the foot of Mount Baldy. I continued my hard work-outs since I wanted to stay buffed and cool, despite the fact that most of my peers were more focused on school. I also started going to the fraternity parties on Friday and Saturday nights and drinking prodigiously. I'd never drank much in high school since I believed that drinking killed your brain cells and made you fat from the empty calories. However, in college, like in high school, I desperately wanted to fit in, and the "coolest" guys and gals all went to the fraternity parties. Just like with weight lifting, I overdid it. It wasn't enough that I had a few beers on a Friday night. I had to be the best drinker at the party. Sounds like total ridiculous folly now, but at the time I was consumed with being cool. Cool in my mind meant being a student athlete who could get good grades, party on the weekend, lay out in the sun during the week—since, after all, I'd come to California to enjoy the endless summer—and then go to the beach when we all had time. At first, I'd struggled to drink beer, which to me tasted like what I imagined pee would taste like. At the fraternity parties, the beer was warm, poorly carbonated, and cheap. I didn't care about that though. All I cared about was proving to myself and everyone else that I could drink a lot and quickly. Within a semester, I was able to drink eighteen beers on a weekend night and have what I thought was a great time with everyone else. The alcohol liberated my previously shy me. It made me funny. Irreverent. Wild. Crazy. The life of the party.

I never stopped to consider if anyone else around me was drinking eighteen beers. I never stopped to consider if I looked foolish chugging one beer after another. Shotgunning them. Pounding them. Drinking them right-side up from a beer bong. Drinking them upside down from a beer bong. It was this last way of drinking beer that I was literally better than anyone else in the school at doing. The upside-down beer bong, as we called it, was made possible by standing on your hands while two other people helped you. One held your legs up, so you could balance yourself, while the other person put the tube from the beer bong in your mouth, so you could chug the beer while upside down. The key to drinking the beer effortlessly, I discovered, was relaxing your throat, so the beer just went down to your stomach without you trying to gulp it. I'd first discovered the trick when I'd rushed one of the fraternities my freshman year. I spit up some of the beer the first time because I had been nervous, tried to chug the beer, and could not keep up with the speed of the beer zipping down the tube. However, the next time the older fraternity brothers lifted my legs up, I focused all my energy on relaxing my throat so the beer would slide down it. It had gone amazingly well, and low and behold, I became the fastest upside-down beer drinker on campus. I loved getting my buddies to lift my legs up in the middle of a party, and then I'd guzzle the beer down faster than the other guy next to me as everyone chanted with glee, "Chug, chug, chug!"

In college, I got the nickname Z-barbarian, which I thought was really cool. Having been a pencil-necked kid at the beginning of high school, I thought that it was supercool that I was now the big guy on campus. I wore tank tops to show off my bulging biceps and my great tan; I studied secretly in the library for hours so that I could appear supersmart in my economics classes while partying on the weekend. I made it all look effortless, and I was idolized for it. Girls wanted to date me. Guys wanted to hang out with me. Professors liked my easygoing style and the fact that I aced their exams. I thought that I had it made, particularly because my parents had helped me buy a used BMW 530i. I raced around campus and to the beach listening to Billy Idol at full volume, thinking mainly to myself how great things were going. How awesome my life was. Dreaming about forming my first company. Becoming an entrepreneur. Having a huge house on the beach in Hawaii. Windsurfing every day after I slayed the gods of business. My life, I thought, was going awesome. And in many ways, it was, although I didn't realize that the hard partying, carb-loaded eating, and fixation on lifting weights would later cause real damage to my body and psyche by the time I was about to turn forty.

"I normally skip breakfast," I told the doctor sheepishly. I knew from my father that not eating breakfast was the wrong answer. However, one thing I'd always been good at was telling the truth to others.

"Well that at least partially explains what I'm seeing here," the doctor said while looking at my charts. Again, the doctor was talking cryptically. I wished that he would just tell me what he had to say. What was wrong? Why was he continually staring at his charts? I began to feel a bit annoyed that this visit was taking so long. All I knew so far was that something was wrong, but I didn't know what.

"What do you normally eat for lunch and dinner?" It was such a simple question that I took a moment before I responded. This visit wasn't going like anything I had planned. I imagined that I was going to come in, the doctor was going to touch my chest and back with a stethoscope, check my reflexes by hitting my knee with one of those small mallets, and tell me I was in pretty good shape but just had to shed a few pounds. I'd added the weight so gradually over time, and I'd replaced the muscle with fat so slowly over time, that it had never occurred to me that I was 50 pounds overweight. My broad shoulders hid pretty well the fact that I had a "tire" around my stomach, as my weight-lifting friends liked to call it. Being a CEO in my thirties meant that people around me treated me with respect and never really told me anything negative about myself. I was living my dream that I'd dreamed in high school. I was a Silicon Valley entrepreneur. I'd married a beautiful Brazilian triathlete. I'd raised millions of dollars from venture capitalists. Forget the fact that it was all coming crashing down around me—I still had a positive self-image that hadn't changed that much since I was in high school. I was the all-American athlete, scholar, entrepreneur, and Renaissance man. I could do everything and make it look easy. In college I'd studied in secret. Now I would lie awake at night, unable to sleep and then get up while my wife was asleep and work for hours on an investment presentation I needed to make in order to raise my next round of capital. And raising capital had been super hard. I'd literally spoken to over two hundred investors and been turned down two hundred times. For the mere mortal, I thought, they would have been crushed by failing to secure capital after so many conversations. Like everything that had preceded me working to raise capital, I just took this on as another challenge. Another thing to conquer to show how great I was at life. At being cool. At having it all. The American dream, or at least my distorted version of it.

I sheepishly told the doctor about my late-night martini drinking, which had gotten more frequent as the pressure built up. My late-night pizza eating. I'd found a place on the way home from work that had incredibly large and delicious slices that I could wolf down in less than ten minutes. While I knew eating late-night pizza wasn't great for me, I rationalized the fact that I had just worked a twelve- to fifteen-hour day. It was my treat to myself for all that hard work. For being willing to be the CEO when my two co-founders had cowered away from the position, not wanting to shoulder the stress. And like always, I told myself that I would burn it off in the morning. I was just carb loading a bit at night, which as long as I ran in the morning would be a good thing. It would give me extra energy. Make me feel strong. All was good. Particularly if I mixed a martini or two or three in.

I further told the doctor that I loved to hang out with my engineers for lunch. I loved to bond with the team. While I wasn't an engineer myself, I thought like one. I'd been trained at McKinsey & Company, the elite management consulting firm, after college on how to solve complex problems very analytically. How to break them down into pieces. How to take almost any subject that I knew nothing about and quickly and systematically determine the root issue and the sub-issues that sprang from it. So now I was an entrepreneur hanging out with a bunch of engineers who were also highly analytical—albeit applying their smarts to coding versus building complex business models. I didn't want to be the "weird guy" who was eating salad for lunch while they were snarfing down burgers, so I ordered burgers, too. While I was at it, I ordered some fries and a Coke to go along with it. I mean, after all, hadn't all the fast-food restaurants that were growing around the country like crazy taught us that this was the all-American meal? A burger, fries, and a Coke. Few things seemed more American. More basic American goodness. The simplicity of what made America great.

Like me, most of the engineers were in their mid-thirties. All of them were overweight and had bodies that looked nothing like the young lanky boys they had once been. Most of them walked with their head jutted forward with their super-logical big brains directing them through life. Their bodies looked like pears. They all sat at their desks for eight- to fifteen-hour stretches, coding while they looked at black screens that had green letters zipping across it as they added code. They were the worker bees that made this new thing called the Internet possible. I was their CEO. The architect of our collective dreams. Building a business model and slide decks that showed how the mobile social network we were building was going to change the world. Our slogan, which was terrible in hindsight, was "Your Life in Real Time." I loved it because it summed up how I lived my life. In the fast lane. Making fast decisions. Being bold. Being a leader. Working hard. Partying hard. Being one of the guys. But also being *the* guy. The one they all looked up to. The one that they talked about when I wasn't there, or so I thought they did.

I mean, before I became a CEO, all I could think about was how cool it would be to become one, and I spent hours analyzing the guys that I worked for. How they conducted themselves in meetings. How they effortlessly told a funny joke when they started to present their slides before turning to the important business at hand. How, they raised millions of dollars from venture capitalists. How, as titans of the new digital economy they were literally remaking the world. From a world built around primarily low-skilled labor to one built around knowledge workers who were building all sorts of cool and fantastical things online. Forget the fact that none of them, including my start-up, made any money.

The doctor was gaining steam now. The depression seemed to lift, and for a moment he was back to his former shelf. A brilliant doctor who could pierce the veil of his patients' BS and cut to the root of what their health issues were and help them see simply what was wrong and what they needed to change.

"Do you see here on this chart these numbers?" he asked. I stood up to get a better look at the charts he was looking at. There were a series of numbers that the doctor explained were my "vitals." Since he knew that I liked math, he said that these numbers were a simple way of representing how well or poorly my body was doing. They were the basics that anyone who goes to the doctor often gets measured. Your heart rate. Your blood pressure—both diastolic and systolic. My cholesterol level. And a few more biomarkers that I can't remember now.

I pointed at my heart rate, which was under seventy and which I thought was pretty good. Clearly, things weren't that bad. He said that it was true that I had a good heart rate but not a great one. The issue was that the trend was bad and going in the wrong direction—up. Even though I hadn't been to a doctor in years, I had gone to the same doctor as a kid and as a teenager, so all my vitals had been stored at my previous doctor's office. Before I'd come to see this doctor, he'd asked me to get the pediatrician to send him all my health records. And he was right. While my heart rate now was just about seventy, it had been in the mid-fifties when I was in high school. My blood pressure had been ridiculously low when I was younger. While 120 over 80 was what was considered average, when I was in my teens my blood pressure had been 105 over 67 or something close to that. Now it was 140 over 100. We reviewed similar trends across all my vitals. The punchline was that they were all going in the wrong direction, and from what the doctor could tell by talking with me, I was living an extremely poor quality of life from a health standpoint. I wasn't sleeping enough, I was eating carb-laden foods, I was drinking too much, I was sitting in a sedentary position for hours, I never stretched, and I exercised in fits and starts—oftentimes pushing myself too hard given the fact that I was 50 pounds overweight. It was the last part that gave me pause. Fifty pounds overweight? Please! At the most I was 20 pounds overweight. I'd been 210 in college. All muscle. Now I was 230 and a little bit softer around the middle. The next stat the doctor showed me was that my muscle over the past twenty years had been replaced by fat. It hadn't helped that I'd bulked up by weight lifting over the years, since that muscle had now turned to fat and my total body fat content was close to 30 percent. Thirty percent? Are you kidding me? When I was a younger, my fat content was in the low teens. My blood pressure was going up as he read one stat after another about how things were heading toward a bad place fast.

"It's really your choice," he said. "You can either change your diet dramatically, or the alternative is turning forty and letting entropy take over." I asked him to translate that into simple English for me.

He told me bluntly, "You're fast approaching obesity. Two-thirds of Americans are overweight. One-third are obese. If you continue on your current path, you could not live much past fifty."

CHAPTER 2

Shine: Your Moon Shot to Happiness: The Shine Paradigm

I sat at home by myself after the doctor's visit. I was stunned. Afraid. Worried. Trying to rationalize in my mind that the doctor didn't know what he was saying because he was depressed. His wife had just died, and he could barely keep it together himself. I mean, I exercised at least three to four times a week. Things couldn't be that bad. But secretly I knew he was right. It was harder to walk up the flights of stairs to my San Francisco apartment. I struggled a bit to get out of my chair after a long session at work. When I ran, my legs and felt really heavy, like I was carrying a large weight on my back. Talking to someone on the phone after I climbed up my apartment stairs, I was always out of breath. Struggling to get my wind back. As someone who had run three marathons, I knew the difference between feeling great and feeling not well. Feeling like your body was decaying and falling apart.

The problem was, I was hungry at the moment. I had the urge to eat something and to eat it now. Mainly because I was hungry, but also, as I would later learn, because I used food as my therapy. To make me feel good when things weren't going well. To control my stress. To treat myself after pushing myself too hard at work. To smooth over the fact that my wife and I weren't getting along.

Vanessa and I had met eight years earlier when I was living in LA, working for an Internet services company as the Head of Business Development. She was a stunning woman from Brazil who had been a former top five triathlete and top ten cyclist from her state of Espirito Santo. She was also a biochemist/pharmacist. I had been wowed by her when we first met, because she combined, like me I thought, the ability to be both an athlete and an academically inclined professional. What I would soon learn was that the two of us were not even in the same league when it came to athletics. There was a huge gap between me, the weekend warrior athlete, and Vanessa, who had gazelle-like legs that carried her at a speed that blew past me, especially in my 50 pounds overweight state.

We had met at a bar called the Circle Bar. It literally had a horseshoe-shaped bar where Santa Monica hipsters gathered around to drink in the dim light at night. I had gone there solo, which I had done with increasing frequency as my buddies couldn't keep up with my hard-partying ways. And I was on a mission to meet a girl. While I had been shy when I was younger, becoming the head of business development had given me a false confidence. To sell the company I was working for. To sell the services we offered. To sell myself. As a math-driven guy, to me it was all about numbers. How many sales calls did I make a day. How many of those sales calls resulted in leads. How many of the leads translated into sales. I figured getting dates with women was the same way. Instead of putting pressure on myself to meet and fall in love with just one, I would use my "business development logic" to meet tons of girls in order to reach the right one. My math was pretty simple—if I talked to ten girls a night, seven turned me down, and three gave me their number, I was off to a good start. Then if I called all three girls and one said yes to a date, then the night had been a success. If I did this over and over, in no time I'd have more dates with amazing women than I knew what to do with.

So, there I was at the Circle Bar practicing my logical but perverse logic. I cringe now, remembering how I slowly circled the bar, talking to one woman after another, oblivious to the fact that the latest woman probably had just seen me get blown off by the woman right before. The alcohol-induced haze meant that the farther I got around the bar, the drunker I became. As a Head of Business Development, I'd learned that it was important to make it more about the client than about yourself. So, I'd start a conversation with an attractive woman by commenting on her cool hat. Or I'd ask her if she'd ever been to Europe. Or I'd just go up and say hi. My theory was that the key to being successful with women you didn't know was to act natural, act like you did know them, so they'd let down their defenses. To some extent I was right, despite how crude and inefficient my tactic was. However, to me, I was grounding what I was doing in basic psychology.

My mother was a psychologist who, when I was younger, had practiced using Freud's psychoanalytic technique. Understand a person's past and you could predict what was wrong in their present and how to correct their future. This theory went well for me since, while at the time I wasn't a deep thinker, the basic idea was that if I got to quickly know a few things about a person's past, then I could make all sorts of assumptions about who they were now, make some witty banter with them, and if I was lucky, get their number. More on my mom and our complicated history later . . .

Unlike most other guys at bars who spend all their energy trying to get women to go home and sleep with them, I believed I had a superior strategy. All I was going for was getting the girl's number. Why? It had a much higher probability of success. It put the woman instantly at ease that I wasn't trying to get her in bed. I had always been good at discipline. Separating the short-term goal from the long-term goal in order to maximize success.

I was about halfway around the horseshoe-shaped bar, and I was having a horrible time. While talking to girls when half-drunk had never been particularly great for my odds, normally by this point in the evening, I would have gotten at least a few numbers. Tonight, however, I'd gotten none. Many of the hipster women had simply ignored me. Others had refused my offers to buy them a drink. Yet a few more chatted with me for a moment or two, realized I was inebriated, and then turned away. Things clearly this night were not going to plan.

Right as I was about to make the turn to go down the other side of the horseshoe, I spotted Vanessa. She was standing by herself at the makeshift dance floor. She stood out from the rest of the women in that she was wearing a long dress. She looked elegant. Like she was radiating some sort of magical light, I thought in my alcohol-induced daze. I put on my best Zoolander "blue steel" look, took a long sip of my icy cold vodka soda, and as casually as I could muster sauntered over to talk to Vanessa.

I introduced myself, asked her about herself, and before she could tell me much about herself, I announced to her that I was a vice president of business development. I proceeded to give her the top three bullets of my resume. I had graduated with top honors in economics, I had worked at the world-famous consulting firm McKinsey & Company, and I now worked at one of the top Internet services agencies in LA. I'd told her all these things to impress her, since when I had asked her about herself, she had said she'd come to the US to be a biochemist/pharmacist. Wanting her to know that I was not just some drunk guy approaching her, I'd shifted into what I thought was my professional self, despite the fact I was at least six or seven drinks in and had just blurted out a bunch of facts about myself. She looked at me for a long moment and then smiled gently at me. Years later, before we got divorced, Vanessa would tell me that she had considered walking away right at that moment, because she thought I was being a pompous ass, and in Brazil, no one would ever dare to walk up to a stranger and brag about themselves in such a brazen way. In her culture it was rude. It was low class. It was the equivalent of asking a woman her age. Asking your boss how much she made. It was something simply not done.

However, right before she turned away, Vanessa considered that she was in the US and perhaps things were different here. Maybe this was how American men acted. While the truth is that oafish American men do act this way, many do not. However, she didn't know this, smiled, and said it was really nice to meet me. After I blundered through a few more things about myself, I realized that this woman had not walked away and that there was something different about her. She was warm. Friendly. Unassuming despite her impressive accomplishments. By that point in the conversation I knew she was a former professional athlete. She also, I kid you not, seemed like she was radiating light. It was something about her eyes. They literally sparkled. Even today as I look back on that night, I know that there was something different about her. My friend Glenn, who later on got to know Vanessa well, said that if there was such a thing as fairies, Vanessa definitely was one who flitted about the world sprinkling fairy dust on people like me who needed help. When I asked for her number, she gave it to me easily. It was so easy that I wondered if there was something wrong. Had she not understood my question? While she spoke English amazingly well, she hadn't been in the US that long. She wasn't even supposed to be at this bar. She'd only gone because her friends wanted to go, and they convinced her she needed to go out and meet some Americans. Unlike me, Vanessa didn't like to drink. She liked to move. Be active. Be healthy. And had only come to the bar because her friends told her that she could dance. She'd stuck out dressed as an upscale, elegant Brazilian compared to all the dark and grungy-looking hipsters that filled the bar. I got her number, unlike how I normally did things, walked straight out of the bar, not trying to get more numbers, and went home rather than trying to get more numbers.

Back to present, the hunger still hadn't gone away and Vanessa wasn't home. I went to the refrigerator and looked inside. There were all the vegetables, beans, and rice that Vanessa had cooked the night before and would eat tonight for leftovers. Then there was the pizza box that still had a few cold pepperoni slices left in it. That's what I craved. That's what I wanted more than anything else. However, I was scared. Literally by what the doctor had said. Despite how obvious it was that I was overweight, no one had told me I was getting that fat. Vanessa, the always over-polite Brazilian, said that I looked good when I asked her. My friends didn't say much because they were also drinking hard and starting to get pear-shaped bodies of their own. Having a doctor an hour earlier tell me that if I didn't change my diet, I likely might not live past fifty scared the bejesus out of me.

Like many times in my life, I decided abruptly and without much more thought that my new goal was going to be to lose that 50 pounds as fast as possible. No matter what it took. How painful it was. This was my new challenge. This was my new North Star. This was going to be my path to happiness. What I didn't know at the time, but know now, was that this simple, single decision would change my life. It would lead to me being more successful than I had ever been previously, and with more grace and less effort than before. Sure, I'd still work really hard to create the successful, multimillion-dollar business I run today. However, it would be much easier to create this business because I was clearheaded and not in a processed-carb and alcohol-induced haze.

What follows in this book is my journey from being a guy who hit bottom at forty to a guy now who is genuinely happy. Sure, I, like everyone else, have my bad days. My ups and downs. My share of failure. My share of my wife, Christina—an amazingly strong and funny woman whom I married after I put my Humpty Dumpty life back together—putting me in my place when my ego goes unchecked. However, compared to where I was, I'm in a markedly different place that all started, like all good personal growth stories do, when I realized that I had a problem, threw the pizza box away, and began to clean up my life.

Before I tell the rest of my story, I want to pause for a moment to share what I call My Moon Shot to Happiness, The Shine Paradigm. It's taken me the past ten years to figure out an approach to living that has transformed my life for the better, and I hope that if even a few principles resonate with you, it could help yours as well. I want to make clear that I did not discover any of these ideas overnight, nor are many of the ideas uniquely mine. Instead, as I tapped into the collective wisdom of enlightened souls around me, I used my left analytic brain to put a paradigm around my approach to personal fulfillment and my right intuitive brain to help me find my way. So, without further ado, here it is:

THE SHINE PARADIGM

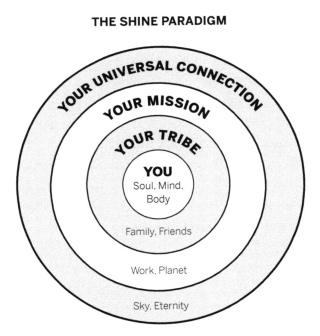

The first thing you probably noticed looking at the Shine Paradigm is that it's made up of four concentric circles with the first one being all about you. However, it doesn't stop there just you, but places you in the larger context of your tribe, your life mission, and ultimately your universal connection—what frees you and creates what I like to call your Eternal Sunshine or Bliss.

Over the next few chapters, I will do a deep dive into each one the aspects of the Shine Paradigm as I tell my story. While each one by itself has had a powerful impact on my well-being, it is the collective sum of them all that has resulted in my path, for the first time in my life, toward genuine happiness and sustained success that feels easy and natural. To living a life that doesn't feel so intense. To living a life where doing well and doing good can coexist. To living a life where success still takes really hard work but doesn't always seem just beyond your reach. To being in the present. To valuing your loved ones. To making an impact. To truly setting yourself free.

Before we dive into the deep end of the pool, the following chapters of this book, I've provided a short overview of the Shine Paradigm for people like me who like to have a quick roadmap of where they're headed before they take off on a journey. However, if you prefer surprises versus punchlines, then I'd recommend you immediately skip to chapter 3. Otherwise, carry on.

You (soul, mind, body)

As the son of a psychologist, I believe that it all starts from within. From your soul. From your North Star. The age-old question is, What is the soul? Is it divine inspiration from an almighty God? Is it a collection of electronic impulses between the neurotransmitters in your brain based on a biochemical reaction? No matter what you believe, what I believe is important is that it's your Inner Voice. And the moment when you calm down your overactive mind and start to listen to it, you'll start to feel less lost in the world and know which path forward is right for you. While this sounds easy to do, when most of us are honest with ourselves, are the opposite we are absolutely terrified by what our Inner Voice might tell us, since it never lies and often the things it tells us to do are the opposite from a career or relationship standpoint of what we're currently doing. However, the moment that you stop listening to your Inner Voice, or what's more commonly called your intuition, you'll find yourself not feeling centered. Feeling lost. Overwhelmed by decisions. The good news is that it's easier than you would think to connect to your Inner Voice. You just have to actually let down your defenses and listen to it.

Once you have your North Star, the next most important thing is to be mentally strong. While many people, myself included, want to jump past focusing on our mental state to focusing on succeeding at our job or whatever our goal is, that has never worked for me. Sure, I'd have spurts where I'd be super productive at work, but then I'd get bored or distracted and my work would suffer. I found it hard to keep up the pace at work. To have the energy day after day to be "on." To focus on what is most important. To make quick, effective decisions grounded in dreams versus fear. Moreover, while it sounds ironic, I found that the way to become a warm, giving person on the outside was to become a mental warrior on the inside. What does that mean? Simply put, to put on your "Big Boy" pants in life and come up with a set of reachable, exciting goals that if you attained them would make you feel proud inside to attain. Importantly, these are not goals to impress others or to fill your resume. You're not trying to get into Harvard or be written up in *Entrepreneur* magazine if you achieve these goals—although accomplishing them may very well lead to this. Instead, the list of goals you come up with, what I call your Life Bucket List, are the things that you secretly know, from listening to your North Star, or would make you happy as you achieved them. Finally, gaining inner mental strength means not listening to all the naysayers when they tell you that your dreams are crazy, unrealistic, too risky. No, when you have fortified the warrior within you, your relationships you'll quickly realize how much energy these naysayers are sucking out of you. You'll start to cull down and make new friends who, like you, are positive, passionate fellow dreamers grounded by concrete goals and the action plans to achieve them.

You may have noticed that I titled this section "soul, mind, body"—in that order. While many books you've read probably put them in a different order, I believe that it's only after you have your soul and mind in harmony that you can focus on your body. When it came to my body, I spent most of my life taking it for granted. Using it. Abusing it. Not really thinking about what it was or what it meant to me. But if you stop to think about it for a moment, our bodies are truly miraculous things.

Take the example of lifting up your hand. Seems like something pretty basic, right? But that one simple act requires millions of electrical signals to be sent from your neurotransmitters through your nervous system down to your hand to tell it to move, and then you have a feedback loop back to your brain once you create the action that tells you what you touched was cold. Hot. Smooth. Wet. Pleasant feeling. Something dangerous to avoid. I now have a toddler son, Max, and watching him day by day learn to smile, roll over, crawl, walk, and now start to talk feels like watching humanity unfold. Like watching *2001: A Space Odyssey* where the early primate humans learned what fire was. To use sticks. To heal and fight with one another.

Once I slowed down and started to appreciate how amazing my body was, it led me to an obvious second decision, which was that I wanted to do everything in my power to take care of it. Because for years it had taken care of me, and now it was time for me, like a child taking care of its parent as she ages, to take care of my body. While exercise definitely has continued to be important for me, it was the moment that I started to eat clean, healthy food that I truly transformed my life. When I stopped drinking the sugary soft drinks. Just said no to another Coke, fries, and burger meal. When I replaced late-night martini drinking with morning sun runs. When I embraced Food As Medicine.

Your Tribe (family, friends)

For anyone who doesn't live on Mars, it will come as no surprise that part of becoming your best self is building a support group around you, what people in some societies call your tribe. As obvious as that sounds, I spent my twenties and thirties so deeply wrapped into my brain that I was pretty much oblivious to the world around me. It created a distance between myself and my family, particularly my wife at the time, Vanessa. Everything revolved around me. My work. My success. My wife. My friends. It never occurred to me that I wasn't the center of the universe. That I was part of a tribe as opposed to these people just being tentacles of an octopus called me.

While I'm a huge believer of independence (getting your soul/mind/body together) before interdependence (family, friends), I've come to learn that investing in and nourishing your tribe is just as important as nourishing yourself. The question is how to do that if you're the type of person like me that has spent a large part of their life trapped within their mind versus connected with others. While there are a bunch of my life lessons I'll share with you, I'll give you a hint. It all starts with a hug—the heart on heart connection between two people who love each other.

Your Mission (work, planet)

So, this is where things start to get interesting. For some who read my book, I imagine you'll think, *This is what I've been waiting for. You said you lost 50 pounds and built a multimillion-dollar business now worth close to $1 billion. Tell me the simple steps to do that, and I'll be on my way!*

Well I have good news and bad news. The bad news is that there is no formula to success. Having studied literally hundreds of successful peoples' life journeys, the one thing I'll tell you is that they are all different. However, at the same time, the people that I admire most are all united in a similar way: They've found a path to doing well by doing good. What business schools now like to call "social impact businesses." A double bottom line. A mission-driven business. Connecting what you're doing at work to how it impacts the planet. Sounds simple, right? In many ways it is, but only after you have the tools to make the right decisions, since the moment you become the CEO of your own life, you'll feel incredibly liberated but also realize that awesome responsibility. My three favorite quotes related to work and our responsibility to our planet are:

"Courage is grace under pressure."
—Ernest Hemingway

"To those whom much is given, much is expected."
—John F. Kennedy

"Earth provides enough to satisfy every man's needs, but not every man's greed."
—Mahatma Gandhi

Your Universal Connection (heavens, eternity)

The final concentric circle of the Shine Paradigm is your universal connection. While you, your tribe, and your mission are all important, I found that it was my connection to something larger than myself that ultimately gave me a true feeling of happiness and freedom. While I have never done it, my friends tell me that when you take the herbal drug ayahuasca, you get this amazing feeling that you are connected to everything. That you see the connections between your life, the lives of your loved ones, the people you work with, the animals, wind, rain, mountains, and air around you. After all, at the molecular level we're all made up in different amounts of the same raw materials. No matter how different we all look on the outside, on the inside we're all similar. We're all bound by a life force greater than ourselves. Some call this life force God. Others ascribe it to the Big Bang theory. No matter what your religious beliefs are, our life force is the ability to truly feel your connection to something greater than the mere matter around you, which I've found ultimately creates the feeling of true happiness and peace.

In the final section of my book, I'll discuss a truly amazing experience I had in my early twenties that saved my life. However, it wasn't until I was older that I realized how miraculous this life experience was. How it changed my life forever. For the better. At the time, using my logical brain, I just reasoned that when I fell off a cliff and didn't die, it was because of a set of logical reasons versus the idea that there was something looking out for me. And that something was right inside me, not way up in the heavens.

While becoming a highly successful Internet entrepreneur was my dream in life, it has been my newfound openness to connect to the mystical and magical around me that has transformed my life and to those individuals who are most happy around me.

Before you toss this book aside and say, "This guy sounds like a new age nut," you should know that nothing could be further from the truth. I didn't grow up religious, I shunned new age ideas when friends and family members shared them with me, and I've always been a skeptic by nature. However, to limit your entire existence to your five senses and not take part in what shamans call your sixth sense would be to deny yourself some of the great wonders of life. As one of my good friends once said when I asked him why he believed in God, "life is more interesting believing in God than not believing in her."

While I still don't believe in God in a traditional sense of a fatherly figure with a long beard looking down on us, as many religions have promulgated—from the Greek mythology of Zeus to the Bible's Yahweh—I find the idea that we're all part of something much larger than ourselves I find terrifically exciting. Here's a simple question: If you view yourself as an intelligent human, wouldn't life be much more fulfilling and worthwhile if we lived in a universe that was intelligent as well?

However, reaching your Eternal Sunshine doesn't mean being naïve. There are countless terrible things that happen every day around the world. Terrorism. Racism. War. Famine. And many more. Connecting to the greater life force around us doesn't mean ignoring these things. Quite the opposite. It is realizing that we're all connected. We're all in this together. That their happiness is ultimately our happiness. When the planet is sick, we are sick. When others go to bed unfed, then when we go to bed fed it's unsatisfying. As someone trapped in my own head the first forty years of my life, I can humbly say that I am a neophyte compared to the masters like Gandhi and Buddha who intuitively knew at an early age the truth to these statements. That said, when I changed my life to focus on those beyond myself, I became much, much happier. As I enter the second half of my life, I literally feel like I'm starting to shine. From the inside out. I hope my story will help you find your path, and as Pink Floyd's lyrics say, "Remember when you were young, you shone like the sun. Shine on you crazy diamond."

CHAPTER 3

Soul: The Cosmic Monkey Business of Finding Your North Star

I call this chapter "Cosmic Monkey Business" because finding your North Star can be really hard for people like me who have been trapped in their heads for years. For analytic types, it seems silly to even discuss something called your soul, your Inner Voice, or your intuition. Because how do you measure it? How do you find it? How do you nurture it? How do you know that it is even real? To an overly analytical person like me, the idea that we have this unknowable, undefinable thing called a soul totally seemed like monkey business. It seemed like cosmic gobbledygook. It was something that I'd ignored for years to my own detriment. It was only when I learned to embrace and listen to this cosmic monkey that I began to gain confidence and happiness in life. But more on that later . . .

When I was in college, I decided that I was going to be the most rational person on the planet. I was going to let reason dictate all my major decisions. All my key turning points in life. Sort of like an Ayn Rand character on analytical steroids. I studied economics, loving the central idea that what made the market work was that it was rational. It was based on what I thought were the immutable laws of supply and demand. Of each person acting perfectly rationally in their own self-interest. However, even in economics, as I got further into it, I realized that it was not totally based on reason. One of the most fanciful elements of Adam Smith's *The Wealth of Nations* was this notion of a magical "Invisible Hand" that is what guides the market. Which sets prices. I also read another economist named Charles Fourier's economic philosophy. He believed that if you could measure everything, then "one moon would become six and the sea would turn to lemonade." It was heady, and in the case of Charles, crazy stuff that made me start to reconsider my total analytic man hypothesis. However, I wasn't ready to change anything yet, and every time I had to make a decision, I would reason for hours about the pros and cons of the various options. Was it better to go into business for myself post-college or join a consulting firm? What were the pros and cons? Was it better to study abroad or not?

Raising logic to the ultimate pedestal helped me land the job for the ultimate rational dude—an analyst position at the top consulting company in the world, McKinsey & Company. After eleven interviews where I answered case study after case study about things I knew little to know about, but where I logically reasoned how I would derive the answers, I was given a job to work out of their LA offices. To say the least, I was over the moon, since it was considered the best job you could get out of college back in the early '90s. My parents, who had grown up in the '70s and were former hippies, wondered aloud if I was going to be what my mom termed "a glorified bean counter." Bean counter or not, I was going to work with the titans of American business. My singular focus on being an analytic man, I thought, was paying off big time.

Not surprisingly, while being Mr. Analytic Man worked for a while as I entered my new life as a newly minted management consultant, over time it left me feeling empty. Lost. Without a clear direction in life. Sure, I could analyze any situation almost too deeply. But what did it all mean? How did all these discrete analyses I was doing add up to anything greater? Working on business study after business study using my sharpened analytic skills to answer questions (like was it better to reduce 15 percent or 20 percent of a department's tea—which I learned in the business world that you could conveniently dehumanize by calling FTEs—to maximize profitability?) Left me feeling a deep lack of purpose in life and a hollowness that was hard to fill.

Luckily for me, I'd been raised by former hippies, and deep down in me there was something yearning to break free. This something I'd later learn was my Inner Voice that I'd muted for years and ignored. It was my soul, desperate for the oxygen of real-life experience and feelings versus just one antiseptic analysis after another. One night, after working for nearly two years at McKinsey and feeling totally burnt, I had a simple yet powerful revelation. A thought popped into my head that, while many problems were hard, few were truly interesting and worth my time. Looking back, at twenty-three that was a pretty prescient thing to decide. It had been helped by the fact that one of the last consulting projects I did was in an abandoned downtown LA building—studying for a major oil company what the optimal gas station should be like. After months of analysis and running regression after regression, one of our lead analysts sheepishly told the partner that the only statistically significant variable in our data was that if the gas station owner had a German last name then the gas station had a higher likelihood of being successful. Not only did that sound racist but it also sounded downright silly, especially given that the client had paid us hundreds of thousands of dollars to come up with a vision for the gas station of the future. While we ultimately told the client something much better than that insipid insight, I finished the project with a feeling that I had just spent the last six months of my life working twelve- to fifteen-hour days on a problem that, in the scheme of things, didn't matter at all.

In contrast, when I was in college at the liberal arts school, we'd spent our time discussing terrifically important problems. How and why some economies grew and why other developing countries struggled. The trade-off being efficiency and fairness in a fast-growing economy. During my senior year, I'd written my thesis on the pros and cons of the US and Mexico border maquiladora industry, where foreign companies operated in Mexico and shipped products to the US. I struggled in the paper between discussing how these foreign companies increased wage rates for Mexican workers, what clearly could be viewed as a good thing, and at the same time that these factories took advantage of Mexican workers by US standards. It was fascinating, heady stuff that made me realize, as a privileged young American, how well off we had it here and think about how many things needed to be fixed in the world.

However, after two years of post-college work at the management consulting firm, I felt lost. Dispirited. Tired.

Burnt out. I struggled to imagine how I could spend the next thirty years of my life working on problems that, like I said before, were complex and hard but seemed in the greater scope of things not to matter. Too focused on profit with very little focus on the projects' impact on real people. On the planet.

I had no idea what I wanted to do next. The one thing I knew that I didn't want to do was to go to business school. While many of the best people that today work at my company, Sun Basket, went to some of the best business schools in the country, after two years of mind-numbing spreadsheet crunching (including *Tron*-like dreams where I zipped between Excel spreadsheet cells all night long), I needed a change. But what to do?

I'd spent my entire childhood dreaming about being an entrepreneur, and now two years of working in the business world had soured me on business. On building model after model about businesses I cared little about. On building PowerPoint after PowerPoint, telling stories about businesses to which I had no connection. In hindsight, I can tell you that my reaction to consulting was a bit melodramatic. Frankly, I wonder today, given what I know now, if I could have found an artful and thoughtful way to change my reality within the world of consulting so that it was meaningful, since there are amazing, intuitive consultants that use more than just reason to help business leaders solve important problems—which are much more interesting than gas pump configurations. However, at the age of twenty-three, it was the fierce organ rejection of my self-created analytic man that sent me on a wild journey with many crazy, unpredictable turns as I attempted to find my place in the universe. What mystics would call my life force, more commonly known as my life purpose.

I returned home from McKinsey and spent a summer with my high school friend Tom going out and drinking every night. Our drink of choice was the Hurricane, a really strong drink from New Orleans with a lot of rum in it. Having just spent the past two years in analytic overdrive, it felt good—at least momentarily—to let things go. That is, until I woke up to my mom screaming one morning. I'd evidently passed out while peeing after a hard night drinking. As I passed out, I'd fallen and hit my head on the toilet seat, and my mom had found me lying next to the toilet with blood oozing out of my forehead. Luckily, I wasn't seriously hurt, but I did have to have a long discussion with my mother where she painfully asked me what she'd done wrong when I was a child, given that I was drinking so heavily now. Not wanting to have anything to do with what I perceived to be psychobabble, I reassured my mother that she'd done everything right and I'd slow down my drinking and be more careful. Later I would realize that my mother and father's divorce, particularly her midnight escape from the East Coast to the West Coast with me in tow as a five-year-old and without my father's knowledge had had a dramatic impact on my life. However, at the moment, I had no interest in introspection. I just thought I was blowing off steam and having a good time with my old buddy Tom.

That summer I got another shock to my system as my mom and my stepfather, Mike, announced that they were getting a divorce. While I had understood why my mom (the mercurial psychologist who grew up in a rich family) and my biological father, Bert (the introverted, workaholic scientist who grew up poor), hadn't worked out, I was shocked when my mom and my stepdad, Mike, sat me down and told me they were calling it quits. It literally turned my reality upside down. While my post-college life at McKinsey hadn't gone as planned, I came home thinking that I would rebalance myself by reconnecting with my childhood that I spent with my mom and stepdad, whom I deeply loved and respected. Finding out that one of them had cheated on the other, that my mom was now following a new age guru who called himself Lazarus, and that my little brother was lighting things on fire in the house freaked me out. Like any overly analytical person, I tried to reason with my mother to stop being so new age, since it was pushing my stepdad away from her. I asked her, what would she prefer to have—her new age beliefs or her family? I asked my stepdad why he was leaving. My mom had supported him when he was down; shouldn't he do the same while my mom was going through what we both believed was a false spiritual enlightenment? I was surprised by the level of anger and resentment he had bottled up toward my mother. The same with the rest of my family, as I quickly learned that according to everyone all around her, my mom was the source of the marriage's problems, my stepdad's problems, and my mother's brothers and sisters' problems. While I didn't buy this, my rational brain didn't see a good solution.

And like any young man who didn't want to deal with conflict, I moved out. First to my grandpa's big home up on the hill by the University of Utah. My grandfather the entrepreneur. The creator of radio and TV stations. The Cable Hall of Fame entrepreneur, with Bob Magness, had created TCI, which hired John Malone and later became Liberty Media. He was and is one of my idols. Like me, he'd later become undone by his own analytic brain that came up with false assumptions,   to make a really bad decision. That would destroy the amazing businesses he'd worked so hard to create. But more on that later . . .

While sitting up at my grandfather's home, I considered what to do next. The obvious answer would have been to go work for one of my grandfather's businesses, since I'd enjoyed working there during my college years. However, I was too proud to ask my grandfather if I could come back. Further, I wanted to strike out on my own. Do my own thing. While when I was thirteen I wanted to be an entrepreneur and I still deeply respected my grandfather, the two years at McKinsey had left me totally burnt out on the business world. So, I decided, at least for the short term, that wasn't for me.

Instead, as I was eating mint ice cream while sitting next to my grandfather, I made one of the first truly intuitive decisions in my life. I decided that I was going to be a writer. A writer? You must be wondering where that came from? That was the antithetical opposite of my analytic businessman vision of myself. However, that was the idea that popped into my head. I ignored the idea for a few days, but it simply would not go away. As I had a bunch of free time on my hands, I'd spent time reading and re-reading some of my favorite books, sitting on my grandfather's deck overlooking Salt Lake City. *The Heart of Darkness. The Dharma Bums. Fear and Loathing in Las Vegas. For Whom the Bell Tolls. Narcissus and Goldmund.* A whole grab bag of books where courage, daring, and, more importantly, the importance of something greater than just analytics played a huge part in the characters' lives. Gave them purpose. Gave them a direction in life. A through line for their journey.

Despite having no training in writing outside of a few English classes in college, I decided that what would give meaning to my life was to become a writer. To follow my idols like Ernest Hemingway. Fitzgerald. Conrad. To live a life full of adventure. To get rid of the corporate shackles. To boldly proclaim to the world that I was an artist. To put my analytic brain in its place. It was a moment where, for the first time in years, I thought that I'd found my North Star. My reason for being. I felt so excited that I immediately called my girlfriend at the time, Anna Elsy, who was in Puerto Rico visiting her family, and told her she needed to move back immediately so that we could both follow our dreams—mine to be a writer and hers to be an actor.

Surprisingly she didn't tell me no way. Instead, she said that she had been thinking about the same thing. However, given how analytical we both were, we decided that we needed to go take classes on how to become a writer and an actor, respectively. Looking back, I now realize that the choice to become a writer or an actor is a monumental decision not to take lightly. It implies taking a road where there are no right or wrong answers. It implies likely sacrificing making a good living while your friends become doctors, lawyers, businessmen and -women. However, I felt for the first time I felt truly liberated from the business world, which I felt had all but eaten my soul away.

The question was where to go to take these classes and start our journey? Instead of picking an obvious city like New York or LA, I did what I'd always done and overcomplicated things by doing a consulting-style seventeen-point analysis of what location in the country had the best playwrighting and acting courses where you could be a non-matriculated student. My analysis had all sorts of things in it like the cost of living, the community's investment in the arts, the number of writing and acting programs in the area, etc. After an exhaustive analysis of ten different major cities in the US, I selected Minneapolis, which in hindsight was both a great and wacky decision like any decision made purely based on logic without letting intuition also play an important part.

The good reason for selecting Minneapolis was that it had terrific writing and acting programs for non-matriculated students, i.e., community courses where you were automatically admitted, which was good for Anna and me since we didn't have artistic portfolios to show. I ended up at the Playwrights' Center and she ended up at the Guthrie Theater. The deficiency in my over-analytic approach was that I'd missed the obvious. Neither of us had forecasted how ridiculously cold Minneapolis was in the winter. When I picked Anna up from the airport after she flew in from Puerto Rico, I was stunned that she was wearing a miniskirt and high heels when it was minus forty degrees outside and the roads were covered with ice. She, too, was shaken by how cold it was, coming from one of the most beautiful, tropical places on earth. Even though I'd grown up in Utah, I'd had no idea of this kind of cold either.

To support myself, I met a woman who would become a mentor and second mom to me for life—Judy. She was a former McKinsey consultant who ran her own consulting practice and was working for a large bank in Minneapolis. My routine became doing analytic consulting work for her in the morning and then doing my writing in the afternoon.

This sounded good in practice, but I immediately began to favor spending more time doing the analytic work, which came naturally to me, and to procrastinate doing the creative writing work afterward. Further, the more classes I took at the Playwrights' Center, the worse my writing became. I became fixated on the structure of plays, including theme, plot, subplots, and character development. Instead of writing naturally and intuitively, I would spend hours building consulting-like diagrams of the plots and how they related to the subplots. I kid you not that I spent more timing graphing the emotions of my characters than writing about these characters' emotions and feeling them.

Like any good journey full of twists and turns, we decided as a group—Anna, Judy, and I—to leave Minneapolis one afternoon after I'd been bitten by a huge mosquito. While I had toughed out the winter cold, the huge mosquitos in the summer sealed the deal for me that it was time to move. More importantly, New York City meant big city, big lights to both Anna and me, and Judy had spent her adult life working in NYC and loved it as well.

I enrolled in New York University's screenwriting program— by now I'd decided that movies, not plays, were the thing for me, and I proceeded to write an incredibly terrible screenplay called *The River of Diamonds*, which was my bizarre take on Joseph Conrad's *Heart of Darkness*, told through the lens of a Mormon mission gone wrong in Indonesia. While the premise potentially could have been interesting, and I had some relationship to the story as someone who had grown up around Mormons in Utah, I'd never been to Indonesia, I'd never been on a Mormon mission, and I didn't have knowledge or emotional connection to write a story so foreign to my own life story.

Despite how bad this screenplay was and despite my immaturity as an artist, I decided to double down on my filmmaker path and move to LA. I applied to and was accepted into UCLA's prestigious MFA program in Film Production/ Directing. In hindsight, it's shocking that they let me in, since my work wasn't very good and I didn't have a clear artistic vision of where I wanted to go. However, I think when UCLA's admissions team was interviewing me, they believed they'd found an oddity. To use the cliché, a diamond in the rough. A guy who'd grown up doing hardcore business—I can't remember, but I think I showed up to the admissions interview wearing a blue suit and wingtip shoes—whose favorite movie was Scorsese's *Taxi Driver*, and who had written this bizarre, deeply flawed screenplay that had Oedipal themes. In fact, my guess is that it was after I started to cry when one of the professors asked me about the Oedipal theme in my script and they learned of my difficult relationship with my mother that I caught the interest of the admissions board. It showed there was something real and human behind the veneer I tried so hard to put on for the world.

By this time, my relationship with my mother had totally devolved. She had gone from being a well-respected psychologist in the Utah community to divorcing my stepfather, Mike, and moving to California where she could follow her new age guru, Lazarus. Quick Internet research showed that her guru was a former ad sales executive who, like many charlatans peddling hope for a living, had created an alter ego, Lazarus, which he claimed to channel for my mother and his other disciples' benefit. My mother had stopped practicing psychology, was quickly spending what was left of her inheritance on Lazarus, and even stranger yet, had opened an ice cream store with her new age friends, which was rapidly losing money when I looked at her accounting books.

I guess the admissions officers thought that the combination of a disaffected young businessman mixed in with a son that had major mother issues might make for an interesting filmmaker, and they took a chance on me. Out of two thousand applicants, I'd been selected as one of twenty students into one of the most prestigious film schools in the country.

I arrived in LA ready to start anew again and become a famous filmmaker. And here's where things started to go off the rails. The teachers and kids in UCLA's graduate film program were really smart. Super cerebral with sophisticated artistic vocabularies. With really impressive artistic backgrounds much stronger than my own. While—with few exceptions—none of them were great artists, they knew bad art when they heard and saw it. And the stuff I was creating stunk. It was clichéd. Forced. Not original. Not funny. Racially insensitive without meaning to be. And I wasn't alone. Our classes felt like verbal sparring matches as these super-intelligent students tore each other's ideas apart. Like a therapy session gone unhinged. Students telling other students that their work was trite. That the characters where two-dimensional. That my male character would be more interesting if she were female. For the first time in my life, even more so than at McKinsey, I felt truly lost.

The North Star I'd clung to so fiercely after leaving the business world disappeared from sight. I had no idea what I was doing in film school. I felt like a terrible failure. I knew my work was bad. And I did again what I'd did my whole life. Instead of listening to my intuition, I done anything but that. I asked others for their advice and followed it, even when deep down I knew their suggestions were wrong. I analyzed and re-analyzed my stories, tearing them apart and starting over and over again. I drew graph upon graph to chart my characters' journeys instead of listening to my characters' voices and letting them tell me who they were and where they wanted to go.

I left film school after having created a few student award–winning films but feeling like a miserable failure, since I didn't trust myself to know what was good and bad. Because I wasn't listening to my Inner Voice and was instead totally preoccupied with what other students thought of my work. Surprising as it may sound, I didn't spend a week working in the film business despite having spent over four years in graduate film school, but instead immediately went back to the world of business, working at a leading Internet services business.

Like any decision in life, this was neither entirely good or bad. On the good side, I lucked into joining the digital economy right as it was getting started, and it's been a terrifically exciting twenty-year journey that has brought me to where I am today, running a leading online healthy meal delivery service that has more than 1,700 employees, services 98 percent of the US, and went from zero to $300 million in revenue in less than four years. However, the bad part back then was that I felt like I had abandoned my dream to be a writer and filmmaker instead of following it after graduate school. And why did I stop? While you can't blame your life decisions on others, I did have a conversation with my father that changed my life trajectory away from film and back into the realm of business.

Upon graduating, I'd gotten an unpaid internship with the product company of Penny Marshall, of *Laverne & Shirley* fame. When I told my father, I thought that he would be really proud. Instead, my hardworking, overly analytical scientist father yelled at me over the phone about how he'd told me that film school was a waste of time, how he couldn't believe that a graduate student of one of the top film schools in the country couldn't even get a paid job upon graduating, and how the world of film was essentially a scam for wannabes like me. Instead of telling my father that he was wrong, that internships were a normal rite of passage in Hollywood, I called Penny Marshall's company and told them I could not accept the internship.

Instead, I found a listing for a fast-growing Internet company, interviewed, and quickly got the Director of Strategy position, and called my father back to proudly tell him that I now had a job paying $75,000 a year two weeks after graduating. While my father was thrilled and I desperately sought his approval, inside I felt like a terrible failure, having taken my seven-year journey from when I left McKinsey through film school and, in my mind, tossed it in the garbage without even trying to succeed as a filmmaker.

I know what you must be thinking. Why was it that black and white? Why didn't I just do the Internet strategy job during the day while I made movies at night? Great questions for which I don't have a great answer. However, like many artists and athletes who I have met who once they couldn't devote 110 percent to their work they quit, I did the same. It was one of the costliest emotional decisions of my life, since for the first time I told myself that I had failed. That I had quit. That I was too chicken to follow my dreams. That the seven-year run-up to this point had all been for nothing. I'd never felt farther away from my North Star. My Inner Voice, which had been so clear to me up to this point became muted. Confused. My mind raced in a million directions and didn't know what to attach itself to.

Sure, on the outside I looked like the all-American success. I bought a Porsche and raced around LA in it. I rented a cool condo by the beach. I dated attractive, witty women. But inside I felt like an abject failure. It was this feeling that led me to start drinking again—something I hadn't done much of since college. It was this feeling that led me to start eating without any regard to my health. While I made a great decision when I married Vanessa, the amazing Brazilian I'd met at a bar in my alcohol-induced haze, I then proceeded to not give the marriage a chance. I was gone all the time working. I still stayed out with my friends every night drinking too much. I was a guy's guy who, in hindsight, made her feel totally alone. While we lived in the same apartment, it was as if we were in two different worlds.

Fast forward three years into our marriage, and I convinced Vanessa to move with me up to San Francisco to work for one of my best friends at an online hotel booking company. By now I had completely forgotten about film, I was making close to $150,000 a year (double where I'd started), and I was shooting to make over $200,000 a year working for this new firm as the Director of Partnerships. I was in charge of a $100 million business where I worked with online sites where we provided them a hotel booking engine their customers could use to make reservations. They got an affiliate fee for every transaction their customers made using our booking engine, and we made money on each transaction that went through our system. While it could have been a really exciting role if my mind was in the right place, by now I felt totally unmoored, I'd left film, left LA, was absent in my marriage, and was starting to get fat.

Right before I turned thirty-five, I decided that it was time to get things back on track. I was terrified after abandoning my film dream about what to do next. However, I knew that if I kept working year after year as a BD (short for business development) guy that what little was left of my soul would be utterly crushed. I was also desperate to show my then-wife Vanessa that I wasn't a total pansy and could follow my dreams, since she'd met me when I lived in LA and was pursuing the "film thing." I gave myself until midnight of the New Year right after my thirty-fifth birthday to make a decision about what I was going to do next. It could either be a feature film, start a business, or become a venture capitalist. Why I put the last one on the table. In hindsight. I have no idea. I had no background in investing, and I'm not a naturally patient person who enables others to go live their dreams and do things—I like to make stuff myself. More importantly, I wasn't qualified to be a venture investor, outside of my background of being an analyst early in my career.

Luckily for me, I took that last one—being a venture capitalist—off the list and focused on whether to go back into film or to finally start my life as an entrepreneur. What I would later learn is that these two options were not that far apart, but at the time I didn't know that. I obsessed over the decision and really struggled with it. One day I was going to do a film. The next I was going to start a business. Then next I was back to film. I had all sorts of ideas for each and no clear idea which one was the right one.

If this theme is now sounding familiar, the clear problem was that I was not listening to my intuition. My higher self. I was not letting my inner compass let me know what was right for me versus what was right for others. I went around to everyone and asked them what they thought I should do instead of settling myself, connecting with the guide within us that instinctively knows where we want to go, and following that direction.

I drank more. I gained weight as the decision date, the second before midnight of the New Year, got closer. I'm sure I must have been super difficult to be around, because I noticed

Vanessa started to be home less. I wrote down on paper all the pros and cons of the two different options. I analyzed and re-analyzed why one path was better than the other. I asked other people for advice and then got upset no matter which direction they recommended, since it always felt unsatisfying. Finally, and literally ten seconds before Vanessa and I rang in the New Year, I quieted myself down and it came to me. In an instant. The right decision was to start a business. To follow the dream I'd had since I was thirteen to become an entrepreneur. To follow in my grandfather's footsteps. It was a terrifying step in yet a new direction. But I was sure it was the right one. My mind felt clear. My decision felt pure since it came from a place of utter calm. A place of tranquility—my soul—that up to this moment I had been surrounding with complete, self-inflicted chaos. It was a decision that would change my life yet again. Set me on a new course.

Outside of having a child, Max, with my current wife, Christina, it was the bravest decision I'd ever made. One that would change my life. Initially for much worse, but over time to something much brighter and more fulfilling. I was thirty-five years old, and for the first time in years I'd listened to my Inner Voice, and it had told me what was next. I was to become an Internet CEO and entrepreneur. I had no idea yet of how I'd do it, but I was absolutely sure about the fact that this was the right decision. Now I just needed to figure out what business I wanted to start, how to raise venture capital, and how to convince a few other crazy souls to join me on my first Silicon Valley adventure.

CHAPTER 4

Mind: Magic Tricks & Mental Toughness: Building Your Warrior Within

"If you have built castles in the air, your work need not be lost; that is where they should be. Now put the foundations under them."
—Henry David Thoreau

So now I had made my decision to become an entrepreneur. The dream I'd had since I was thirteen. What could go wrong? I thought. Well, not surprisingly, almost everything. The first and most important challenge when you start following your dreams, when you start following your intuition, you'll be surprised how many people come out of the woodwork to question you. I call them naysayers. The negative space in life. The opposite of your inner light, your inner life force.

They'll give you all the reasons not to do it, like my father did when he scolded me for accepting an unpaid position with Penny Marshall's production company. They'll warn you that it's financially dangerous. That other people have already done your idea. That they know what's best for you. That they are on your side. Here to help you make the best decision for yourself. While many people are too afraid to follow their own dreams, they have no problem telling you exactly how you should approach your own life.

And this is where mental fortitude comes in. What I call "building your warrior within." No one is going to ultimately help you stick to your dreams but you. No one is going to tell you not to quit after an incredibly hard day. To persevere on. Quite the opposite. Your family and friends, while meaning well, most likely will tell you the opposite. It's okay to go get a regular job. It's okay not to take risks. Actually, it's better not to because when you take big risks, well, that means that you can lose big. What they never tell you is that when you don't take risks, when you don't follow what's in your heart, you take the biggest risk of all—which is not becoming who you are meant to be. Sounds like new age gobbledygook, right? I'm sure many times in this book you'll think this. Well, maybe it is, but I can guarantee you that it was realizing the power of my Inner Voice, listening to my intuition and not being ruled by analytics, that has helped me in the past four years to create a company that is now worth close to a billion dollars. But more on that later . . .

So how to create the warrior within? It's what Thoreau called your foundation, which is needed after "you have built castles in the air."

Talk to any good entrepreneur about their business, and they will tell you that they take highly calculated risks. They did not become successful purely because they just followed their intuition, but rather, they reached success by combining their intuition with the mental toughness that's required to make hard decisions about which way to take your business or whatever creative project you decide to embark upon.

Flash back to when I was thirty-five and had at the stroke of midnight decided that I was going to become an entrepreneur. What an exciting decision! What a glorious life path awaited me, full of all sorts of interesting turns. Some good and many not so good. But before I could get to the life turns, a thousand decisions first needed to be decided. The most important one was what business I was going to start. In chapter 8, I'll discuss the Entrepreneur's Dilemma: The $100M Business Model. It provides for people thinking about starting a business in Silicon Valley, it details some of the most important questions you need to ask yourself to become successful. However, at age thirty-five I didn't know any of these questions, and I did what many entrepreneurs do—I found someone who passionately wanted to make a product and became the businessman who helped raise the money for it.

I'd met Braxton Woodham when I was in my twenties, working as the head of business development at the Internet services company I previously mentioned. He was an amazingly brilliant technologist. I remember after interviewing Braxton for the job of Director of Engineering that I told my office manager that, while I wasn't a technologist, Braxton was the first truly analytic engineer I'd interviewed after speaking with dozens. I left out the part where Braxton had told me that he was obsessed with green frogs. Like I'd later learn about most brilliant people, they are by turns part genius and part nuts. And I mean that in the most positive way.

Braxton and I became fast friends at the Internet services company called kpe. We wanted to do what Braxton called "bleeding edge" technology for all the major entertainment studios since we were working in LA, smack dab in the middle of Hollywood. However, we quickly realized that the studio captains and their underlings were more interested in basic websites that promoted their movies versus immersive 3-D online entertainment experiences.

One day, Braxton came into my office and said that he was quitting. I was devastated because he was the one person in the office who made the experience exciting. Fun. Not totally monotonous selling entertainment websites over and over. I asked where he was going, and he said it was to a small new company that made ringtones. I'd never heard of a thing called ringtones and asked him what they were. He described that they were fifteen- to thirty-second clips of popular songs that people could use to replace the "ring" on their mobile phones. Not wanting Braxton to leave and thinking that it was a really small idea, I told Braxton that was the dumbest idea I'd ever heard.

Braxton, like any good mental warrior from within, thanked me for my perspective but told me he was going to do it anyway. He had a bunch of ideas of how to build what he called a "mobile media platform" much more powerful than the ones that existed at the time on carrier networks. Note: To date myself, this was at the beginning of the 2000s, before you could even surf the Internet on your mobile phone. I wished Braxton well and told him that as soon as the ringtone thing failed he was welcome to come back to the Internet services company. Braxton thanked me but told me that wasn't likely. I'll always remember what he said next when I asked him why. He said that he wanted to make products. He wanted to create things. He didn't want to be a service provider following the whims of others.

At that moment, I felt a tinge of regret for telling him that going to the ringtone company was stupid. I also felt totally jealous, since the whole reason I'd gone to film school, before I'd given it up to be practical and gone back to business, was because deep down I loved making things. Coming up with ideas. Creating something new. Whether it was good or bad. Producing instead of consuming. However, I was too scared after my brush with what I viewed was failure at film school to tell Braxton anything other than good luck.

Within weeks of Braxton joining the ringtone company he was sending me enthusiastic emails about how well it was going. In the first week they sold a few thousand ringtones. Then the next week it was over ten thousand. Then they had gotten their first carrier, a major mobile company, deal. Then a second carrier. Then deals with all the major music studios. Within six months they were selling hundreds of thousands of ringtones, and within a year it was over a million. I couldn't believe something as simple as a fifteen- to thirty-second clip of a song could be so popular, but there was no doubting the incredible sales figures Braxton would email or share with me when we hung out. I decided the next time Braxton had an idea, I wouldn't tell him it was stupid since, wow, he'd hit a goldmine in ringtones—something I would have never guessed would work.

Flash forward to 2004. I had stopped working at the online hotel booking platform company and was working for Braxton's new mobile media company as a gun-for-hire consultant. After the huge success of ringtones, Braxton's company had been bought by the current eight-hundred-pound gorilla in the mobile media space. The new management team was not as entrepreneurial as the team before the company was bought, and Braxton was having trouble getting his new projects off the ground. As the guy who had architected the first cross-carrier mobile media platform that allowed users to turn their rings into ringtones, he now wanted to democratize media. He wanted to make it such that mobile phones could share pictures and videos seamlessly across web and mobile. That mobile phones could play music on them. That you could surf the web using your mobile phone. Buy things. Book your hotel. Research where you wanted to travel. All on your phone. Sound familiar?

However, in 2004, Braxton was way ahead of his time. His new bosses told him to stay focused on ringtones. That was the money maker. That was the proverbial golden goose laying the golden egg. He should stop wasting his time on these newfangled ideas where there was no proven business model. Left unsaid was that there had been no proven business model when Braxton's original company's wild-eyed entrepreneurs had created the ringtone sensation in America. No, the new company was run by a group of supersmart, superanalytical guys who ran everything by the numbers, and Braxton knew just the guy who could help break their logjam: me.

Braxton convinced his COO that the company should hire me to come work with him to build the business justification for his ideas around mobile text, picture, and video sharing. Listening to mobile music and buying it on your phone. As obvious as all these ideas sound now, none of it existed at the time, and Braxton knew that just like with ringtones it was only be a matter of time before this new form of mobile media was going to explode and make ringtones look like a tiny blip. However, even he, if you ask him today, had no idea how big the mobile media industry would become.

I was all too happy to leave the online hotel booking business and try something new for multiple reasons. One was that the CEO was an alcoholic. Every meeting started with me bringing PowerPoint slides, which I had worked on for hours the night before, only to have the CEO brush them aside, offer me a glass of wine for lunch, and say that he wanted to talk about life. He wanted to get to know me. Two was that the business was totally flimflam. It was "out of runway," the Silicon Valley expression for out of money, and the once fancy offices had been replaced by a cramped room where the desks were, I kid you not, separate by shower curtains. Three, I was totally bored from selling the same hotel booking engine over and over. And finally, probably the most important reason, I really believed in Braxton.

Braxton and I got to work, and we built business model after business model showing the huge TAM (total addressable market) for these new ideas. Who wouldn't want to listen to mobile music on their phone? Wouldn't it be great to be able to share a funny video with one of your friends on their phone? What about group texting? Sure, SMS existed, but wouldn't it be fun to send out a message that went out to more than one person. Even bigger, Braxton and his engineers had come up with an idea that they called "JDP." It stood for Java Developer Platform, and the idea was that it was a platform that allowed people to buy and sell applications created for your phone. Before the iPhone App Store existed. Braxton thought that no matter what the new company executives thought of the mobile media sharing ideas he was keen on, they for sure would love the idea of building the marketplace for buying and selling mobile apps. I had one simple mission: Build the business model to prove to Braxton's new bosses that it could be a big business.

After months of work, Braxton and I met with the CEO of Braxton's company. After presenting multiple product ideas—including both mobile media sharing and the mobile application marketplace—we were giddy with excitement, since the CEO, who'd started his professional life as a rock guitar player and who'd built his career doing things he told us were way more far out than what we'd proposed, loved our ideas.

We walked out of the meeting full of excitement. We were sure we were about to create the next huge wave in mobile media entertainment. We were sure until we met with the COO and VP of Product the next day and were told that we hadn't been given the green light. Braxton and I were shocked. How could this be? We just had sat across the room from the CEO and he had told us in plain English, not fancy business speak, that he loved the ideas and couldn't wait to see what we came up with next. What the VP of Product explained to us when we looked at him confused was that what he had meant was that the business plans we'd come to him with warranted further investigation. The VP of Product, as the COO nodded, said that what we needed to do next was to create a business model for each idea. I tried to explain that was what we just did. Now it was time to start creating some visual mock-ups of what the experience could be. The VP of Product ignored me, turned to Braxton, and thanked him for the great ideas. He told Braxton it was time to bring on board a GM to help Braxton analyze his ideas. What about me, I thought? Hadn't I just done that? The VP of Product then added, before I said anything, that it was fine if I stayed and helped the new GM of Products craft the business plan for them. What then transpired over the next six months felt like it came straight out of Kafka's *The Trial*. Just as the character in Kafka's book had no idea why he was on trial despite asking everyone, Braxton and I had no idea how to navigate the labyrinth of corporate decision-making to get one of our projects greenlit. We met with the CEO three times at his request, and three times he told us the projects were a go. We were then told three times by his operating team that the projects needed further analysis and modeling, despite the fact that there was only so much modeling you could do when the product didn't exist in the market. For a guy who was way overly analytical by nature anyway, it was enough to make me a nervous wreck. To question my belief in all the good work we'd done.

I still remember sitting across from the head of corporate development. The calm, middle-aged man who'd likely never taken a big risk in his life, asking me in an even-toned voice how I could recommend to a public company CEO to build these new projects when we had no idea if they would work. How I could be sure of any of the assumptions in my model. He asked me in a voice that showed no emotion, but felt totally sinister to me, how I could justify to myself recommending spending money to a CEO when I had no basis of proof for my ideas. I came out of the meeting with this man feeling humiliated, small, and worthless. He had torn down the artifice that I had spent so many years building. My analytic man was nothing more than a guy who peddled a bunch of half-baked assumptions. What I would later realize was that these assumptions were the mooring of all good ideas as long as they came from your intuition and then were later grounded in facts after you built things and tested if they worked or not. However, at the time, I just felt like I'd let Braxton down as the VP of Corporate Development called the COO, told him none of our models made sense, and that it was time for me to go.

While I'd made a ton of money consulting for this company, I felt like I'd just wasted the last two years of my life. Braxton, being the Internet visionary that he was, was furious that the executives had blocked all his good ideas, after he'd done exactly what he'd been asked to do: build business models to justify them. When I confided in Braxton that all the models just had assumptions in them that could be wrong, as the VP of Corporate Development had condescendingly told me, Braxton said that of course he knew that. That wasn't the point. He knew in his heart, just like he'd known with ringtones, that mobile video, picture, and text sharing was going to be big. Really big. It was the wave of the future and he was sick of waiting for the bozos running the company he was at blocking his ideas.

I agreed. I told Braxton about how as the clock struck midnight right at the turn of the New Year, I'd decided that I wanted to start a business. Before I could say more, Braxton said let's do it. Do what? Start a mobile media business that launched all the cool ideas we'd just spent the last two years working on. After all, the big eight-hundred-pound gorilla company was never going to do them. And Braxton was sure he could get a release from his COO, who'd become like a second father. A mentor to him.

I was terrified. Every part of my logical brain wanted to say no, however, in my heart it was a clear yes! Especially because the last time Braxton had told me he was going to do something—ringtones—it had been a mega success. Of course, the answer was yes, no matter how scared I felt inside. I had to do it. Yes, yes, yes, I was in.

We shook hands and that was it. It was decided. Braxton and I were starting our first company together. We didn't have a name yet. We just had a diagram drawn on a napkin. It was a picture Braxton had drawn in pencil of a unicorn, which was one of his favorite animals since it stood for something that could be versus what was just around us. The unicorn was drawn so that it looked poised to fly, and it was shown right in the center of Braxton's hand-drawn mobile screen. Braxton drew a little button at the bottom the screen and titled it "Share." Before every app in the world later added this button.

I'd already been fired by the mobile company, or as they put it, my consulting contract had run its course, and Braxton soon quit as their CTO. While Braxton worked on getting his former COO to bless us pursuing our newfangled mobile media sharing ideas, I did what I'd always done when I was about to start something new: I built a business model and a PowerPoint for our new company and tried to think about how we could get money to start the company, since neither Braxton or I had much money.

The next night, Braxton invited me to meet a guy named Steve who was working in another division of the large mobile media company we'd both just left. Steve was just as smart as Braxton and—I say this in a good way—even crazier. He had black-framed glasses with think lenses that made his already intense eyes literally bug out at you. He'd already built and sold a hit mobile game company in his twenties, and he wanted to do it again. He loved the idea of a mobile media sharing company, and he instantly christened the company "Zannel," which stood for zillions of channels. It was a bizarre and zany name—in hindsight not a very good one—but for guys that had grown up using Google for search, we figured it was just as good as that name. More importantly, Steve had raised millions of dollars in venture funding from Silicon Valley for his last mobile gaming company. He had connections. He knew venture capitalists. He would connect me.

Strangely, neither one of them wanted to be the CEO. Braxton wanted to be the CTO and Steve wanted to be the CMO. They wanted to follow their inner muses and let me be the businessman. Let me raise the money. As a guy who had always wanted to be an entrepreneur, I of course said yes. I had no idea what I was getting myself into. All I knew was that I was terrifically excited about the idea.

Unlike with film, when my father questioned why I would give up a good-paying consulting job to go off and start a company that seemed really risky, I didn't listen to him. I didn't stop what I was doing and cower back into my comfortable little cubicle. While I still had many lessons to learn, I'd learned by the time I was thirty-five the first two. Number one: Follow your gut. Number two: Build you inner mental warrior. Don't let anyone dissuade you from following your dreams. To stop surrounding yourself with naysayers and instead surround yourself with dreamers like yourself. Like Braxton and Steve. Like these two brilliant guys who had invited me to go on a journey with them to build what we believed was going to be highly disruptive technology that would change the world. We couldn't have been more right about the explosion of mobile media on phones. The problem was that none of us had any idea what we were doing and that the sleepless nights, the long hours working, and the constant stress would drive us to the brink of exhaustion. Destroy my first marriage and lead me on an unhealthy path filled with late-night martinis and pizza and afternoons snarfing down burgers, fries, and Cokes. Anything to mask the terror I started to feel inside as everything started to go awry after we raised $6 million in venture capital. But before everything went wrong, what an adventure it was, raising the money right on Sand Hill Road.

CHAPTER 5

Body: 50 Lbs. Lost in 12 Weeks: Food Really Is Medicine

"Holy cow, Braxton, $6 million just hit our bank account."

I sat staring at my computer. On my screen was Zannel's online bank account, showing that a wire had just hit, transferring $6 million into our account. I'd never seen that many zeros in my life in a bank account. Having spent most of my twenties and early thirties zigzagging between being an artist and working in business, my bank account was meager at best. Six million dollars. I said each syllable out loud. Then I waved over Braxton to come check out my screen. Braxton, who'd grown up poor in Tennessee, couldn't believe it either. He'd been raised by a single mom, and Braxton told me he'd had days where there was little to no food in the fridge. Both of us sat staring at what we thought was a ridiculously large amount of cash in our account for what seemed like forever.

Finally, Braxton broke the silence, patted me on the back, and said that was awesome. For a guy who didn't dish out compliments easily, it was the best thing Braxton had ever said to me, and inside I was totally filled with pride. I called my scientist dad looking to share my excitement with him. Instead of celebrating with me, my overly skeptical scientist father said that he couldn't understand why the venture capitalists had given us that much money. We didn't even have a product. We hadn't made money yet. Didn't it make me nervous having to manage that much money? Wasn't I worried about losing it? Wasn't that risky? What happened if I lost all the venture capitalists' money?

That last question I hadn't considered when I raised the $6 million with Braxton and Steve. It had been a crazy ride. One of the stories I remember most fondly was our first meeting with a famous venture capital fund. Braxton had gotten the lead from a friend of his who was a fellow entrepreneur. And the entrepreneur had given Braxton very specific advice. No matter what, don't show up at the meeting with the venture capitalists with a PowerPoint presentation. Instead, just show up with a diagram of your idea on a napkin. It looked bolder. More daring. More entrepreneurial. For a guy like me who had used PowerPoint as a crutch my entire life whenever I was speaking to someone senior, the suggestion seemed like utter lunacy. However, Braxton loved the idea. He said that because it was his business lead, we were going to do it his way, whether I liked it or not. Begrudgingly, I went along with him.

We sat at a small table in a nondescript room of the famous venture capital firm. Braxton and I had driven down early to Sand Hill Road and had marveled at how beautiful it was there. I'd imagined, erroneously, that since Sand Hill Road was ground zero for Silicon Valley, that the street was going to look supermodern. Nothing could have been further from the truth. Sand Hill Road is right next to Stanford University and is surrounded by lush green trees and foliage. It feels like you are on part of a large, amazingly well-manicured university campus, which makes sense in hindsight, since it grew out of its next-door neighbor Stanford.

After introductions, one of the two VCs (short for venture capitalists) asked us to show them what we had. Braxton proudly pulled out of his pocket the crumpled napkin out of his pocket that had the pencil-drawn image of a mobile phone with a unicorn on the screen with a button titled "Share" beneath it. The two VCs stared at the napkin for a long moment. I was terrified. I was convinced that they were going to start busting out laughing at any minute. And then they said something I would never have expected. "Wow this is really interesting. This is amazing," and instructed an associate to go get the other partners to come into the room.

Within moments, there were a bunch of guys all huddled around the table looking at Braxton's napkin. They were asking him questions. How did it work? How did the photo get shared from one mobile phone to another? Did it also work for video? What about music? With each question, Braxton confidently explained in his visionary way how all of this was possible. How he'd already built the largest mobile media sharing platform for ringtones, and now he wanted to democratize media. It was heady stuff. Unlike the bureaucratic mobile media company we had just worked at, this venture firm was comprised of hungry, ambitious big dreamers like Braxton and me. They could sense something big. Braxton looked over at me and grinned. It was his "I told you so" look, since I'd been so apprehensive about coming to a multibillion-dollar venture capital firm and showing a bunch of Stanford and Harvard MBAs our idea on a crumpled napkin.

Right when it seemed that the meeting was almost getting too giddy, one of the partners asked the obvious question, "Do you have a PowerPoint?" A look of terror crossed Braxton's face as he realized that not only was he right that the napkin stunt could pique their interest, but also before these superrational men released millions of dollars to us, they would want to see a business plan before they released millions of dollars to us.

Luckily for us, I'd secretly created a PowerPoint that included a business plan in case the napkin idea didn't go as planned. I confidently pulled out the PPT, gave Braxton my own "I told you so" grin back, and started to share our vision for turning Zannel into not just a big idea but a highly profitable one as well.

Ultimately, we didn't get funding from that firm for a whole host of reasons that don't matter. We also didn't get funding from a bunch of other ones either, as many of them said we had a cool idea, but we were too early, which meant in VC speak that they wanted to wait until we built the product and they could see some initial traction on it. Eventually we found a young fellow dreamer associate— whose friend had created Yelp, a restaurant review app that was taking off— to convince his senior partner to take a chance on us. We shared our vision with one partner, then two, and then to the entire partnership of the venture firm at what they call a GP (general partner) meeting. It was heady stuff, and I came out of the GP meeting feeling like I was walking on air. That I was born to do this. My normal inner lack of self-confidence had momentarily abated since the partners of this VC firm had said they loved the idea. The young associate and his senior partner had called me quickly after the meeting and told me that they were going to send us a term sheet. In Silicon Valley, a term sheet was the Holy Grail for a new entrepreneur. It was a simple document that said that unless they discovered something terrible about our company in the next few weeks, they were intent on funding us. To the tune of $6 million.

Flash forward to age thirty-nine. It had been four years since we started Zannel. While we'd had such an auspicious start, we quickly realized that starting a Silicon Valley company was the most difficult thing that Braxton, Steve, or I had ever done. The VCs wanted to see the first version of the product within two months, and Braxton hadn't even hired the first engineer. Let alone the fact that the last platform Braxton had built, which was much simpler, had taken three times that long. While Steve was totally brilliant and an amazing businessman, it turned out (and he'd agree if you asked him today) that he was a terrible CMO. His creative ideas for Zannel were off-the-chart bad. While Braxton was working on the back end of the site, Steve put up a few quick web pages to tease the public about what was coming. I kid you not, but he put a photo of a fox wearing a T-shirt that read "foxes are sexy bitches" next to a photo of a Zebra and a gooey-looking burger. I told him that the T-shirt slogan was totally inappropriate and not funny. I also had no idea how this related to the mobile media platform we were creating. As a guy who'd never been a leader before, I didn't know how to communicate this in a way that Steve would be receptive to, and he immediately got defensive. He told me I could not shut down his inner creativity. He had to follow his vision for it. I didn't agree, but to diffuse the situation I asked him if he'd come up with a slogan yet. Steve got excited and said that his eight-year-old had. What was it? "Up your channel." Like "Up yours" but adding the word channel to it. Now I think the idea might have been genius, but at the time I thought it was in terrible taste. Finally, I asked Steve if he'd worked with creators to get our first batch of viral videos to share on the site. Steve excitedly proclaimed that he hadn't gotten videos from anyone else yet, but he had made a bunch himself and he wanted to show them to me.

Braxton and I walked over to Steve's cubicle, and he played the videos he'd created for our mobile app when it was ready. They were a bunch of videos of Steve with his shirt off, showing off his hairy chest and saying things like how he liked to scratch himself or that he preferred to slurp his water versus drink it. At one point in the video he licked his arm and then looked and smiled directly at camera. This is a true story. Steve then asked us what he was. I was confused. So was Braxton. Steve excitingly told us that he was a dog in the video. That was the joke. That was what was going to make these videos viral. When people got the joke that a Silicon Valley entrepreneur was not talking about himself in the videos, but instead was acting like he was a dog. As all the bizarre videos on YouTube were just starting to take off, Steve was definitely onto something. However, I was mortified. So was Braxton. It was time to do something. I fired Steve. A decision I would later regret when overly analytical Braxton and I built a service that was technically complex but not nearly enough fun.

The launch of Zannel hadn't been a rocket success. My first press interview had been a disaster, and the VCs were breathing down our necks. Four years later, we had a few million users, which was cool, and had won a Webby for

Best Mobile Social Network. But in Silicon Valley we viewed ourselves as a failure since we were running out of money and the VCs didn't want to give us more. Why? Because we weren't growing fast enough. Other sites had gotten big faster. Our site lacked personality. Our product was too complicated. It was over-engineered. Not consumer-friendly enough.

And I was thirty-nine years old and not doing well personally. All the years of stress had gotten to me. Pitching two hundred VCs for our Series B, i.e., another slug of funding, over the past six months and being told no two hundred times had gotten to me. I'd started drinking martinis every night with my friend Matt. I'd started eating two or three slices of pizza a night on my way home from work. Vanessa and my marriage was on the rocks after years of my being absent and not there for her. She wanted a divorce. Going to therapy had just made it worse since the therapist encouraged us to tell each other all the things we didn't like about each other. With no good guide rails, Vanessa and I said mean things that were hard to take back. We did mean things to each other. Things that made us not love each other anymore.

The only glimmer of hope we had was that Braxton, on the side, had started building a B2B (business-to-business) version of our website. If we couldn't get users to visit our online island called Zannel, perhaps we could get businesses to use the powerful picture, video, and text sharing platform we'd built to share and track their media across the most popular social platforms: Twitter and Facebook. I was terrified of letting go of the dream of Zannel, but the pressure of not being able to raise a new round of capital got to me and I caved. While Zannel was the big change-the-world idea—look at Instagram, which came years later—this new B2B service, which we named Tap11 (from the Spinal Tap expression, "Turn it up to 11" was the safe bet. Because you didn't have to get millions of users. In fact, all you needed to do was to get a few hundred superlarge companies to use and pay for it. Braxton was a killer technologist and I was a superBD (business development) guy from my days working for the Internet services company and the online hotel booking engine. The VCs who'd written off Zannel as a failure said sure, and Braxton and I were off to the races. In no time, Braxton and I had five hundred enterprise companies using Tap11. They loved it. Twitter named it a top three app in their ecosystem. The problem was that our big enterprise clients didn't want to pay us any money for the service. Not because it wasn't valuable, but because we were too early. Paid social media advertising and analytics was still in its infancy. So now Braxton and I had two cool services: A Webby-winning mobile social network that had millions of users but wasn't growing fast enough by VC standards, and a top three Twitter app that had lots of enterprise clients that wasn't making money.

Sitting at home after having visited the doctor who told me that I was fast approaching obesity, I decided no matter what happened to my business or marriage, I had to get healthy. And fast. Not having a life coach to help me learn how to exercise and eat right, I just did what seemed and felt right to do. Like a few times before in my life, I let my inner voice guide me on what to do.

On the exercise side, I came up with a simple idea. I would do overall body conditioning that consisted of one hundred push-ups a day, three hundred sit-ups, and a forty-five-minute run. That was a great goal to set for myself, but at the beginning I couldn't even come close to hitting those numbers. It had been years since I'd done a push-up. I was mortified when I lay on the ground and tried to push-up, my greatly weakened triceps couldn't even push me up one time. Making sure Vanessa and no one else was looking at me, instead of doing a proper push-up with hands and toes to the ground, I did a few granny ones instead. Granny push-ups, unlike proper ones, are on your hands and knees. My first day I got two reps before my arms shook and couldn't do more. The sit-up side wasn't much better. I put my feet under my couch and with all my might tried a sit-up with all my might. I didn't even make it up halfway before I felt pain in my lower back and immediately dropped back down. I had a bit more success running from my apartment toward the Golden Gate Bridge, since running was the one thing that I'd continued sporadically doing while I was in my twenties and thirties. I ran for fifteen to twenty minutes of the run before I doubled over in exhaustion.

On the food side, it was even harder because I'd spent so many years, particularly the last four, eating foods laden with processed carbohydrates. As a guy who's always been an extremist, never one to phase things in gradually, I decided that I was going to go cold turkey. Pizza, burgers, Coke, and fries were out. So were martinis. My friend Matt got really mad at me when I told him that, because I was his main drinking buddy. He'd grown up in Cleveland and believed it was unmanly and impolite to refuse to drink with your friends. However, for the first time in my life, I held my ground because the doctor had really scared me, and I told Matt I'd be happy to hang out with him at a bar, but I would be drinking bubbly water.

Instead of all the junk food, I did what my dad told me for years I should—do, eat real, healthy food. For breakfast, something that I had skipped for years, I decided that I'd eat oatmeal. Why oatmeal? Well it turns out that oatmeal is a great source of even distribution of energy throughout the day. However, I didn't know that. All I knew was that you could buy one-minute oats at the local grocery store, and I liked the idea of something superfast. I didn't care that it tasted like mush as long as it got the job done. For lunch, I found a local Indian restaurant near my work that also could get the job done. The mental trick that worked for me was that instead of looking at the menu and trying to find the thing that looked most delicious, instead as a goal-oriented person I looked for the things that seemed to be the most boring and healthy. I settled on a side of lentils, boneless chicken tikka, and small salad. At my healthy-eating company now, we'd call what I ordered for lunch "clean" food, since it was all from whole, real foods and, to my knowledge, devoid of any chemical additives. It also wasn't laden with processed carbohydrates. For dinner, I did steamed broccoli and had more chicken and sometimes fish. While I'd grown up hating broccoli, it seemed like the healthiest thing I could put into my body without much work.

At first, this diet as you can imagine for someone who'd spent the last twenty years eating junk food felt incredibly hard to follow. The food tasted bland, especially because I didn't add any salt to it. I craved eating a slice of pizza. My mouth would become moist when I'd see one of my engineers eating a burger and fries at his desk. I wanted more than anything in the world to enjoy all that delicious food laden with carbs. It took about a month before my addiction to bad foods started to wear off, and, as my friend Dr. David Katz likes to say, I started to retrain my taste buds. Gradually, real food started to taste good again. I didn't need salt to taste its naturally bold flavors. I didn't crave the carbs as much. Watching someone eat a burger now looked kind of gross to me. The grease that oozed off the top of a slice of pizza no longer looked appealing to me.

Interestingly enough, the easiest thing to stop was the drinking. I'd always wondered whether I had a drinking problem. What I discovered was that I had a social anxiety problem. It wasn't that I was addicted to booze like alcoholics are. Instead, I had severe social anxiety and used alcohol as a social lubricant to make myself seem wittier. More relaxed. What I thought was cooler around the guys. More hip around the women. However, when I finally said enough was enough, I noticed, not surprisingly, how much better I felt in the morning. How much clearer my brain was. It was as though a twenty-year fog had been lifted. Not only because I was not drinking but also because I was sleeping better.

The only challenge I was having was that I still shoveled food into my mouth, which wasn't healthy for my body. I came up with a simple way to fix this: I switched hands and started to eat with my right hand (I'm by nature left-handed). Being a highly quantitative person, I also gave myself the rule to chew each bite of food twenty times. While this exercise over time was a bit ridiculous, at the beginning I found that it was an amazing way to, for the first time in years, slow down. Actually enjoy my food. Taste each bite's unique flavors. What I would learn is that it was also a great way to reduce the amount you ate, since your stomach, when you eat more slowly, naturally tells your brain when you've had enough.

My exercise routine, as I began to eat more healthily and work out regularly, began to go much better as well. My two granny push-ups turned into three granny push-ups, into five granny push-ups, and so on. Within a week I was up to ten granny push-ups. Within two weeks, I was up to fifteen granny push-ups. By week three, I went back to doing a few traditional push-ups with hands and feet (versus knees) pushing me off the ground. And each time I did a few sit-ups, I did my best not to hurt my back. Like anyone getting back into exercise, it quickly dawned on me that part of the problem was that over the years I'd lost most of my flexibility. I'd never been particularly flexible, even as a kid. And now at age thirty-nine, all the years hunched over my desk had made it such that when I bent over I couldn't even touch my knees, let alone my toes. I decided to add five to ten minutes of stretches to my morning workout. Not surprisingly, feeling looser made it easier to do the sit-ups and lengthened my stride.

Running on the trail that bordered the San Francisco Bay, I marveled at how beautiful the Golden Gate Bridge looked spanning the water. It looked like it had always been there. As though it was meant to be more than some manmade invention for our car driving convenience. I loved how good I felt in the mornings not feeling hungover. Feeling fresh. Feeling alive. Feeling like I could take on anything during the day.

As I got healthier, I measured my progress daily on my scale. Each day I stepped on my bathroom scale and then took a photo with my mobile phone of my weight. At the beginning things did not move much. I was 230 pounds. Then I was 229 pounds. Then I was back up to 230 pounds. Then down to 228. I started to feel dispirited, and then a fellow runner I met told me the obvious. That as your body got leaner it turned fat into muscle. And that muscle weighed more that fat. That made me feel better, but I still knew inside that I was carrying around a lot of excess weight. I resisted the temptation to stop eating breakfast and put blind faith in my process, although I had no idea if it would work, of following my daily eating and working out routine, although I had no idea if it would work.

When the weight started to come off after a few weeks, I was shocked that it came off so fast. Every day when I stepped on the scale, I dropped a pound: 227. 226. 225. 224. And so on. Soon I was under 220 pounds. I didn't tell anyone what I was doing, because I didn't want to jinx it. Inside though I was giddy with excitement. While I was still super nervous and upset about the fact that my business and marriage were failing, at the same time something was going totally right in my life.

I felt in control for the first time in years. I had a goal, which was to no longer be fat. To no longer each junk food. To no longer drink martinis. To no longer be filled with self-loathing. And I was surprised how much better I felt after just four weeks of changing my diet and daily exercise habits. No having met many other people who have gone through similar transformations in their lives, I realize now I wasn't inventing anything new, but rather, was following age-old concepts of how to live a simpler, happier, more healthy life. I was doing the things that people do in places in the world that have been called "Blue Zones," where people live to be one hundred. Where the pace of life is slower. Where the only type of food people eat is real food. Where people walk instead of drive to get around. Where there is a focus on the quality of life versus the quantity of life.

After two months, my friends and family began to notice. I'd dropped below 200 pounds and was now, depending on the day, somewhere in the mid-190s. My pants were starting to look too big on me, my belt was now getting close to the last notch, and my extra-large shirts were starting to look a bit like I was in a dress instead of a men's button-up. People at work commented how good I looked, Braxton and I seemed to get along better, despite the stress of us running low on cash, and options in my life began to reappear.

The biggest one was that Braxton had reconnected with the founders of YouTube, and they were interested in buying our business. Before Braxton and I had started Zannel, Braxton had been offered the VP of Product position at YouTube right when it was getting started. He had asked me what he should do. I'd told him that he would probably make more money at YouTube, but if he stuck with me and we created Zannel, we'd have more fun. While I'd been right about the fact that he'd make more money at YouTube, neither of us had any idea that the site would turn into a rocket ship and mint all the early employees millions of dollars when the company was snatched up by Google at more than one-and-a-half-billion dollars. Sure, Braxton and I had had an amazing experience building Zannel together. But there was no way in a million years that Braxton—a kid who grew up poor and was highly focused on financial independence—would have otherwise picked Zannel over going to YouTube. Whenever I even brought up the word YouTube, Braxton would immediately tell me to stop talking and not "poke the bear."

And now, right when we were on the brink of ruin, the founders of YouTube had reached out to Braxton and told him that they were working on a new venture, post selling YouTube, and were wondering if he wanted to join them. Braxton's answer was of course he'd love to join them; however, he didn't know whether he could since he was still the CTO and co-founder of Zannel and, by now, also Tap11.

The YouTube founders really wanted Braxton and graciously said that perhaps there was a way to work things out. I went to a café in San Mateo to meet with Chad Hurley, who of the two founders was the businessman and designer, while Steve Chen was the engineer and technology visionary. I was both super excited and scared to meet Chad, since he is a legend is Silicon Valley. Known for his artistic genius—after all, he was the one who had come up with both the PayPal and YouTube logos. It turned out that he was also a really nice guy who grew up with a regular childhood just like me. He'd come out to California after college to pursue his dream and had answered an online ad to join this small company called PayPal; he later struck out with Steve on their own to create YouTube. The rest we know is an incredible history. Now he and Steve wanted to build a new site that wasn't about sharing new media. They were convinced there was plenty of that. Instead, they wanted to build a site that was all about curating all this glorious content into one place. They had secretly just bought the site they wanted to rebuild to do just that: del.icio.us. It was one of Silicon Valley's most beloved sites, but it had fallen on a bit of hard times, and Steve and Chad had a cool vision to resuscitate it. I told Chad about my background in media—my grandfather starting the early cable companies, my time in film school, and Braxton and my mobile version of YouTube called Zannel. He said it all sounded really cool and he'd get back to us.

Braxton and I waited anxiously over the next few days, by our phones waiting for a call. And then it came. It was Steve and Chad. They wanted to partner with Braxton, me, and the team. They wanted to together build something we all thought was going to be bigger than YouTube.

I felt like the last crazy four years were now all worth it. Things were starting to come together. Three months after I started eating healthy and exercising regularly, I now weighed 180 pounds, 50 pounds less than I had ninety days before. A friend of mine had taught me how to surf, and I was now alternating surfing with running in the mornings. I felt great inside for the first time in years. Braxton and I were working side by side with two of the Internet's most famous entrepreneurs in Silicon Valley. Two of our heroes, even though we never told them that. It was like growing up idolizing Roger Federer and then finding yourself at Wimbledon on Centre Court in the finals competing with him. And you weren't getting skunked. At least not yet.

The only thing that hadn't gone right was my marriage. Vanessa and I had decided after much soul searching to get a divorce. It was devastating for me as a child whose parents had gotten divorced multiple times. It was the last thing I ever wanted to do. It was for her, too. However, we realized that we'd reached a point that there was no turning back. There were things said and done that couldn't be taken back. While I still loved her, it was time for both of us to move on. I'll always remember when I loaded all her possessions into her car, she gave me a teary hug, and then she drove away to go live in Miami. For the first time in years, after work I had no one to come home to. Instead of taking a taxi or riding the bus home. I walked. It was a strange sensation. On the one hand, I felt totally liberated. I could do anything I wanted now at any time. Not that I hadn't pretty much done just that over the past few years. On the other hand, I felt totally alone.

CHAPTER 6

Family: From Hedonism to Happiness: The Importance of Your Tribe

"I'll pay, don't worry about it."

That's what I said when the bill came and Chad reached to pay for it. It was a silly thing to say to a co-founder of YouTube since he was easily worth a half billion dollars, and my bank account was meagre in comparison. However, I thought it was vitally important not to act weird around Chad. Not to let his huge wealth create an awkward gulf between us. It was also a smart decision, because I could tell from some of the early conversations we had that Chad, justifiably so, often questioned whether people around him really liked him or were just sucking up to him to get at his money. Chad paused for a long moment, smiled, and said it was fine and handed over the bill to me.

The first weeks after Chad and Steve bought our company were heady times. I sat next to Chad in the small office on the second floor of a nondescript San Mateo building. Braxton sat next to Steve over on the engineering side of the room. There weren't many people there yet, since Chad and Steve had just formed the new company together, AVOS Systems, and bought del.icio.us and our two companies, Zannel and Tap11. The acquisition had almost not happened because as at the last moment, the VCs who'd totally written off Braxton and my creations suddenly went from fear to greed. A thing that often happens, I would learn over and over, in Silicon Valley. However, Chad and Steve were smart, tough businessmen. They were also represented, as you can imagine, by some of the world's best legal counsel. They told our VCs that it was fine if they didn't want to acquire our companies. They'd be happy to just hire Braxton, me, and the team and give us big fat bonuses. They were building something else anyway, and the main thing they wanted was to tap into Braxton and his team's genius. While that wasn't entirely true, since Braxton and I had built some pretty cool stuff at our last company, our VCs blinked first, and in no time, we were setting up shop at Chad and Steve's new office location. Wow. I'd just sold my first company. Better yet, I now got to join two of the Internet's most successful entrepreneurs on a cool new journey. What could possibly go wrong?

It was a surprisingly small and humble office for the guys who had built one of the largest Internet companies. However, Chad and Steve wanted to recreate the magic of their first start-up. They wanted to go back to their roots as entrepreneurs, before the VCs came in. Before the money men took over. Told them when to raise more money and when to sell. I marveled at how cool it was that Chad and Steve didn't need to raise money. They could self-fund this new company and make it whatever they wanted. This independence was both totally amazing and, as I'd later learn, something that could be really dangerous since it was created in an industry that already had few guide rails—none.

To say that Braxton was over the moon working for his engineering idol Steve was an understatement. Braxton, in a show of fierce loyalty, proclaimed early in the project that he was not going to shave his beard until we had the new site up and rolling. Until we had rebuilt del.icio.us from the ground up and launched Chad and Steve's new vision. Even more crazy, Braxton decided to put a bed in one of the spare office rooms and live in a cramped eight-by-eight room every day until the site was live. He had missed out on the glory of YouTube, and he was going to throw every ounce into making this new venture successful.

Luckily or unluckily for me, depending on your perspective, I had just been dumped by the woman I'd dated after divorcing Vanessa. I'd been totally smitten with this woman, acted like a fool around her, and she had told me at one of San Francisco's poshest restaurants that right now she needed to focus on her career and it'd be better if we were just friends. This after I'd just taken her to Tahiti and dropped twenty grand I didn't have. This after I'd taken her to Paris, France, and tried to act like the big man who could sweep her off her feet, now that I was working with the YouTube founders. The bad news is that I felt crushed inside. Like I wasn't good enough. Like I was tarnished goods after my recent divorce. The good news was that I dodged a bullet. I didn't end up with a woman who would get right up to the altar with multiple men, and then, for reasons that weren't entirely clear since many of them were terrific, decide that they weren't the right one and walk away.

As it related to Chad and Steve, getting dumped by a hot girl had made me again realize that it was important to add steely toughness to my mental warrior within. Not to shut down my emotions, but to stand up for myself. Not to gush when I spoke to Chad. Not to fawn on these famous Internet pioneers. But to treat them like real people. And I could tell that Chad liked this. He respected it. It made him trust me.

After having worked so hard for many years as CEO, it felt weird to be back as the Head of Business Development, working at the company that had just acquired mine. Having worked fifteen-hour days on everything from strategy to fundraising to hiring to product and back again, it was weird to only have one thing to do. To be Chad's business guy. We'd meet on Monday morning, and I'd have everything he'd asked me to do by Tuesday morning. And then for the first time in years, I watched the clock. Not because I didn't want to work hard for Chad. Quite the contrary—it was because I'd literally done everything that he'd asked me to do and there wasn't anything else he wanted help with. I'd check and double check and suggest new projects I could work on. Chad would thank me for offering but say it was cool and just to relax until things really got going.

As a guy that struggled to stay still for a moment, this was even harder than going at full speed. I think I was probably hyperactive when I was a kid. Even though I'd calmed down as an adult, the idea of sitting all day for four days with no concrete goals to work on drove me nuts. So, I did what I'd always done and threw myself into something new: surfing.

I'd started surfing in the mornings with my new friend Ian, a totally buffed Californian who was also a banker. He was funny and cool, like any kid who'd grown up rich and now worked for his father's investment bank. He was the opposite of me in many ways. Funny. Gregarious. Loud. Confident around women. A goof. He was just like me in that he was a terrible surfer and wanted to learn.

Each morning we'd go out at Ocean Beach and get schooled by the waves. For those not from Northern California, Ocean Beach is one of the most dangerous places in the United States to surf. It has a wicked undertow, it's sharky, and the frigid Northern Californian waters are plain damn cold. I couldn't have cared less, because I was wild about this new sport and hanging out with my buffed, cool friend. I'd show up each morning to work with sand in my partially wet hair and Chad would just smile. Or give me a high five. He didn't care. So why should I?

Since I'd been dumped by a hot, career-obsessed woman, I'd kept a pretty low profile on the dating scene. I was too busy surfing and thinking about surfing. Hanging out with Chad at work and doing the odd project he wanted me to complete for him. Everything was going great, or at least I thought it was, but I still felt hollow inside. Lonely. Like something was distinctly missing. And it was. I was living a hedonistic life. One all about pleasure. Not like the boozy pleasure of my twenties and thirties, where it was all about how many girls I could date. How many martinis could I drink. What kind of fast car could I zip around in. No, it was a different kind of Zenlike hedonism.

After selling my business to the YouTube founders, it became all about me. The good news was that I was healthy for the first time in years. I'd lost 50 pounds. Felt good. Did healthy things like surfing in the morning. But it was all centered around me. What did I want to do in the morning?

What did I want to have for lunch in the afternoon? How did I want to spend my evenings? With the newfound money in my pocket from the company sale and my newfound physique from getting back in shape, I started to shop at San Francisco's hip stores and buy cool, form-fitting shirts. Ripped black jeans that had exotic brand names. Spending too much money and acting like I was the man. The guy with no cares in the world. The guy who only thought about himself. The guy who didn't need anyone else. It was all about me. Enjoying myself after all the hard years being the CEO. Being an unsuccessful entrepreneur.

I updated my apartment with fashionable art for which I had no connection other than the fact that it felt on trend. I dressed in the fancy form-fitting clothes that anyone who knows clothes knew were expensive. I drank thousand-dollar bottles of wine at Chad's house out of Dixie Cups. Why? Because I could. I ate homemade pizza from Chad's wood-fired stove when he invited Braxton, me, and the guys over, and his personal chef made us personal pizzas. I barbecued the rarest Kobe beef with Steve up at his pad in Napa.

It was all totally awesome. The successful life that I'd imagined for myself. And it was all totally empty. Weirdly not fulfilling when you get over the giddy excitement of hanging around famous people. Of drinking wine that came from the world's best chateaus. Don't get me wrong. Living among the super-privileged was an amazing experience. A lucky experience that few get to see, let alone do. However, it didn't fulfill me like I thought it would when I was a thirteen-year-old kid. At night before I fell asleep, I felt really lonely. Despite the newfound money and fancy friends, I felt totally lost again.

And then I met Christina. It had happened like most good things in my life, by accident. I had gone to a bar with a bunch of friends, wearing these crazy glittering silver pants called "Discorounds." It's a long story. The short version of it is my friend Chris Lindland had started a cool online men's clothing company called Betabrand. They had become famous for selling all the digital worker bees hip and cool clothes for both work and play. Discorounds had become a megahit at the yearly arts festival out in the desert called Burning Man. Burning Man was a pilgrimage made by many of Silicon Valley's most successful entrepreneurs to go find themselves in the desert. But more on that later . . .

At the moment, I was in a bar with a bunch of good-looking, six-foot-tall-plus guys all wearing glittering silver pants. The excuse was that it was one of the guy's annual reliving of his bachelor party. Why? Because it was fun. It was a wacky thing for a bunch of guys to do. Because the married guy had a cool wife who gave him a hall pass once a year to hang out with his buddies and blow off steam. Put back on the costume of his single manhood and have a few drinks with his friends.

We weren't on the town to pick up women, since many of the guys were married or had girlfriends. We were just having fun. We were at a grungy bar in the Mission neighborhood that I would never have gone to on my own when a really attractive, tough-looking girl came up to my friend Enrique and asked him why we all were wearing these ridiculous-looking shiny pants. They started to banter back and forth, each one outdoing the other one. In no time Enrique pulled me aside and said, "Dude, this is one supercool woman. I can't do anything about it (since he was married) so you should."

Christina still cringes when I tell this story, since it makes it sound like it was a transaction between two men. A hand-off. And to a simpleton like me, in many ways it was. I stepped over to speak with Christina, and Enrique went over to hang out with the other guys. The first thing I noticed talking to Christina was how fast she spoke. Witty stream of consciousness zingers. One quick self-effacing funny story after another. A leap from one idea to the next. Like a kaleidoscope of cleverness that came effortlessly to her. I was smitten from the moment that I met her but didn't want her to know it.

Christina decided it would be more fun to hang out with a bunch of wacky-but-safe guys and told her friends to go on to the next bar without her. We all piled into my buddy Enrique's car, and in no time, Christina had put on a werewolf ski mask that Enrique's kid had left in the back of the car. She was talking to the guy next to me, Bob, and I got worried that she was going to like him more than me. Bob was young, great looking, and had gone to Princeton. However, as luck would have it, Christina and Bob figured out that Bob's best friend had dated Christina's best friend. And it hadn't ended well.

Christina, being the fiercely loyal person I'd later learn that she is, immediately was turned off by Bob, although it was his friend and not his fault for treating Christina's best friend badly, and she turned her entire attention to me. We all went to a funny show in North Beach were there was a cover band playing ridiculously well former-disco hits, which went well with the theme of our disco pants. We then went to play pool at a bar nearby. I was impressed and tried to keep up as Christina guzzled down beer, schooled the Israelis we were playing pool with, and then said she wanted to go eat pizza.

As we made our way, I did what I always did in these types of situations. I tried to impress her. I told her about being a writer. I told her about a recent book I'd read, *The Kite Runner*, which I told her was a terrifically moving book written by a local San Franciscan author. Christina chatted gamely along, but I could tell she was more interested in giving the taxi driver directions to Golden Boy Pizza. While the pizza couldn't compare to pizza she'd grown up with in Chappaqua, New York, we both agreed that it was the best late-night pizza that San Francisco had to offer.

As we stood in line waiting for pizza, Christina took my hand and held it. I hadn't held hands with a girl since Vanessa and I had gotten divorced. Sure, I'd hooked up. I'd had my share of dates. But I hadn't had this one simple act of connection with another human being. It felt innocent. Good. And it made me strangely happy inside. And for a moment not alone.

When we got to the counter, Christina asked me how many slices I wanted. I said one and she let out a loud guffaw. Like I would learn later, Christina wasn't one to suffer fools. She wasn't one to be impressed by guys trying to watch their weight. Be pretty boys. She asked me again if that's what I wanted, and I sheepishly said yes, since I'd recently lost 50 pounds and was terrified of putting the weight back on. And because after losing the weight it had definitely made me vain.

Christina shrugged and said fine. Then she told the guy behind the counter that we'd have six slices. A half dozen slices? What? What was she thinking? Before I could protest, she said that she didn't care if I wanted to starve myself, she was hungry and wanted to eat pizza. So, it was one for me and five for her.

We got back in a taxi and headed to her place. As we drove, I thought that I really liked this girl who had worn a werewolf ski mask, gone disco dancing with a bunch of guys in silver pants, and had just ordered herself six slices of pizza. I didn't want to screw things up, so instead of asking myself up, I asked her for her number. Christina, part of the social media generation, gave me a weird look, grabbed the pizza box, and as she flitted away told me to look her up on Facebook. She'd later tell me that she didn't think I'd call, because no guy she grew up with would let the girl take all the pizza home. She figured that I must be married and didn't want to get in trouble with the wife.

I got home and couldn't sleep. I hunted and searched for Christina and finally found her. She must have told me her last name, since there was no other way that I could have found her on Facebook. On-screen there were a bunch of pictures of her traveling the world, riding on a donkey while she worked for Habitat for Humanity, being goofy with her friends wearing a superman cape, and holding a baby in her lap. It was the last photo that startled me, since when I'd met her I hadn't immediately thought maternal. She had been wearing a motorcycle jacket all night, her wit was razor sharp, and I'd met her at a bar in a rough neighborhood in the Mission. The last image of Christina Card I looked at on Facebook seemed incongruous to the woman I'd just met.

"How was the pizza?" I wrote the next day. She immediately wrote back, "Great for breakfast." It was the perfect comeback. Christina's level of coolness grew even greater in my eyes. That she would eat pizza for breakfast. That she'd tell this to the guy she'd just met the night before. She didn't care what I thought. And I thought that was awesome.

It took us a few weeks to get together for a date, and she suggested an Austrian restaurant that was near where she lived in Russian Hill. I showed up in one of my one-size-too-small John Varvatos shirts. It was a shirt that I could never have worn when I was 50 pounds overweight. Now at a super-slim 180 from eating healthy, surfing, and running every day I thought it looked good on me. Casual elegance. Looking good without trying too hard.

To my surprise, Christina showed up in a below the knee-length orange dress. The total opposite of the leather jacket and faded jeans look from the first time we met. She seemed nervous. A bit unsure of herself. She awkwardly told me while we were waiting for a seat by the bar that she'd forgotten to put on her bra. She called me "superman" a few times as I rattled off story after story trying to impress her. I wasn't sure what to make of being called "superman." Was she impressed by me? Making fun of me? A mixture of both? Why did she seem so uncomfortable? Where had the wit gone? Where was the woman that I had met before?

We settled down at one of the tables and the Austrian owner came over to see how we were doing. Christina very politely told him how this was one of her favorite restaurants and asked him how he'd gotten the idea to start it. While the owner shared his story and Christina listened to his every word, suddenly it dawned on me—I'd met a nice girl. By accident. At a bar that I later learned she never went to either. Wearing a leather jacket that wasn't her normal clothing either. Meeting her on a feisty night when she'd had a "what the fuck" kind of attitude on.

Now tonight, on a date with me, she was nervous. Unsure of herself. Had put on a really pretty orange, full dress to impress me. As though she was going to her high school prom instead of on a date with a guy she'd met at a bar. Instead of being turned off by this, I was actually smitten even more. In my heart, I was a dorky, shy, self-conscious guy from Salt Lake City, Utah, who had spent the last twenty years of his life in big cities. Trying to act cool. Trying to be a hit. New York. LA. San Francisco. The whirlwind of the pace. The buzz of being in the fast lane. The excitement of creating things that had never been built before was exhilarating, but it was also tiring.

I tried to put Christina at ease, because I could tell all my bragging about starting this company and that was making her feel uncomfortable. It wasn't making her like me more; it was making her like me less. Every time she said the word "superman" in reference to me, it wasn't a compliment. It was a way of her saying that I was trying to show off. Be the big man. Be better than everyone else.

I wisely decided to ask her about her family. Like me, Christina had grown up in a family where her parents had gotten divorced. Like me, she'd struggled when her parents separated and moved across the country from each other. She'd been uprooted from her friends. From her home. Just like I had been. She told me all about her brothers and sisters. About growing up back East. About her funniest best friend named Ally and her coolest best friend named Kira. It reminded me of when I was growing up in Utah. Dating girls who felt real. Not pretentious. Just real. The tough New York girl that I'd met first had been replaced by a softer version. A woman who cared deeply about her friends and family. As she got more comfortable around me, the witty zingers came back. The New Yorker inside her couldn't help but make fun of my douchey shirt. My douchey pants. I mean, come on. I was almost forty years old. Why couldn't I just wear Levi's?

Right when things seemed to be going great, Christina said that she didn't feel well and needed to go home. I immediately walked her to her apartment and then she went up the stairs quickly and disappeared. I wondered if I'd done something wrong. If I'd said something I wasn't supposed to say. That night I couldn't sleep. The next morning, surfing with Ian, I couldn't get into a rhythm. When Chad asked me if I wanted to eat lunch with him, I said no. Something I never did since I cherished the moments I got to hang out with him.

And then she texted me. It felt like an eternity. She apologized for not feeling well and wondered when I was free to get together again. I was over the moon. Wow! Life felt grand again. There was this thing that felt warm inside me that I didn't know what it was, but it felt good. I wanted more of it. I was starting to get addicted to this feeling. Whatever it was.

The next restaurant we went to was even cooler than the past one. We went to a hipster spot in the Mission close to where we'd first met. The restaurant was called Gracias Madre, and it had the best vegetarian and vegan food I'd ever tasted. Christina was relaxed. She'd had a great day at work. She regaled me with funny stories about her best friend Ally and growing up together with her. She and her San Franciscan best friend Kira in their twenties trying to pick up men. Of her falling flat on her face after trying to kiss a really cute man. I didn't feel threatened at all, but instead liked her even more.

I did what I typically did in situations with women. I thought the key to her heart was trying to impress her. Show her how amazing I was. I invited her to go watch NASCAR racing in Sonoma—not the regular way by driving to the event, but rather by flying there via a helicopter that Chad and Steve had arranged. I took her to a U2 concert where we had the best seats in the house, provided by one of my good friends who worked with Bono at a private equity firm. I took her to one of my rich friend's ranches for the annual music festival that he held on his property each year. Silicon Valley's version of Woodstock. And I almost lost her.

The more I tried to impress her, the more distant she became. I couldn't understand it, since I'd been wired since high school that the way to a woman's heart, or so I thought, was to impress her. To court her. To woo her. To make her feel like a princess and I was her prince there to save her. Wow her. Make her realize what a good provider I could be. And boy was I wrong. One night, Christina totally lit into me. Told me that I was totally in my own head. Was just focused on listening to myself talk and talk and talk. She couldn't take it anymore. She was sick of hearing all my great stories about myself. What about her? What about what she wanted in life? What about her stories? Did I ever stop and think for a moment what was going inside her?

As the son of a therapist I was deeply embarrassed, because I knew she was right. Had I really changed so much, from being a teenager who loved to listen to other people's stories, that now I was such a full-grown douche that the one woman I was in love with couldn't stand my company? I decided to change and did my best to ask Christina questions, as I was terrified of losing her. The amazing thing that happened is as soon as I shut up, Christina flowered. She told me one funny story after another. She cracked me up. She did wacky things. She invited me to do crazy things with her. It was a whirlwind romance. By far the best of my life. There was only one problem.

Christina wanted to get married and have kids. While I was okay with the marriage part, the kid part freaked me out. Scared me. Made me recoil 100 percent from her. I told her I deeply loved her and wanted to spend the rest of my life with her. However, I didn't want to have kids. For whatever reason, I'd never connected with them. Deep down, I didn't tell Christina this, but I was terrified that if I had a kid, I'd lose my edge. I wouldn't have time to still be an entrepreneur. And it was not wanting to have a kid that almost made me lose Christina.

After five years of going out, Christina was worn out in our relationship and so was I. The start-up with Chad and Steve hadn't worked out, which is an entirely different story; I'd started a new start-up called Lasso that seemed promising at first but then sputtered out; and I was with the woman that I deeply loved but with whom I was terrified of having a family.

Christina and I tearfully broke up, because she said that while she loved me, she wanted to have a family. That was the most important thing for her. She had thought that she could not have a kid, as I'd wanted, but then realized she couldn't do that. All her friends and family had told her that it was time to move on. Kick me off the bus. Let go and move on. I was so incredibly sad and forlorn when she left my apartment and we said goodbye.

For two weeks I moped about my new start-up's office. I wasn't my usual jocular self. I was bummed. Washed up. Angry at myself for not being able to move forward with Christina. Not being able to just say yes to the woman I loved. Because I was too afraid.

I rode my bike to the top of a hill that overlooked the Golden Gate Bridge. I sat thinking for a good couple of hours. And then it came to me. I was being a total idiot. If there was one thing right in my life it was Christina. It was our relationship. It had survived the breakup with Chad and Steve when their start-up didn't work out. Our relationship had survived my current start-up, which was running on fumes, and it had survived the vagaries of my up and down moods that came with the stress of being an entrepreneur.

Christina was working at Google by this time, and I came up with an excuse to visit her office. I walked by her cubicle, and when she looked at me, shocked that I was there, I quickly told her it was for business. She could see right through me and asked if I wanted to go for a walk. In part to talk in private with me. And at least as likely because she didn't want me to create a scene in front of her officemates. Out on the Embarcadero, San Francisco's main drag that runs along the water, I apologized to Christina for our hasty breakup. I said that I missed her. I swallowed my pride. I told her that I was wrong. She was emotional and said that she'd made mistakes, too. She was upset that she'd listened to her friends and family instead of doing what was in her heart. While she still wanted a family, she wanted to work things out with me.

She had to get back to work, so we decided to go out to dinner a few days later at one of our favorite restaurants. A great local restaurant that served amazing Greek food, since Christina was busy with work events this night and the next. I spent the next two days ruminating over and over what I should do. The analyst in me went back and forth a million times. Ask Christina to marry me. Don't ask Christina. The more I thought about it the more nervous I became inside, since marrying her meant the one thing that had terrified me the most. Having a child.

We met at the restaurant called Kokkari, and Christina looked stunning in her svelte black dress. She was at her witty best. She was warm. Funny. Engaging. Loving. Wow. It all came back, before we'd start to fight, how amazing she was. How lucky I would be to spend the rest of my life with her. In that instant, I decided that I was going to marry her. Take the plunge. Do the thing that terrified me most. Start a family with her.

I didn't ask her at that moment to marry me because I wanted to make it special. Unlike my first marriage, where I'd asked Vanessa to marry me on the beach by where I was living at the time, my second proposal was going to be epic. It was going to be just right. The memory I wanted to hold in her and my head forever. And then it came to me. I would ask Christina to marry me in the meadows where my mother and my biological father Bert got married. This meadow was in the middle of one of my favorite ski runs at Alta Ski Resort in Salt Lake City, Utah. First, I had to ask her parents for permission and next find a way to get Christina there.

Flash forward to today. I'm forty-nine years old. I asked Christina to marry me under the sun on a beautiful Utah day up in the Rocky Mountains, and we got married in my favorite place on earth—a remote beach on the island of St. John in the Virgin Islands, and more importantly, we've started a family and live in Tiburon, California.

I have a nineteen-month-old boy named Max, who is the most magical little man that I've ever known. While the nine months leading up to Max being born where some of the most nerve-racking moments of my life—because I was terrified that perhaps I wouldn't connect with him—from the moment he was born I was even more smitten by him than I thought Christina was. If that's possible. The moment he was born, I exclaimed, "Wow, he looks just like me!" Christina, despite just having given birth, gave me a smile. I realized in that moment that for the first time in my life, I had my own tribe. I had a reason for being. It was time to get my life in order. To fix my start-up. To be the best person I could be in my marriage. To be a great father.

I, of course, have days that go up and down. I have things every day that challenge me at work to keep my cool. Christina and I, like any two intense people, get into fights. But never to the point that we step away from each other. Away from our marriage. Away from our family. Away from Max, who has become the center of our universe.

This was a first for me, and if you haven't done it, then I recommend when you are ready—and only then—to make it a first for you. Having a child has made me feel immortal for the first time. Connected to the grand thing called life. Made me have a clear purpose in life. Which is to pass on the knowledge that I've learned to my son. To do what my mom and dad, albeit imperfectly, did for me. Which was to raise me. Help me learn to love others. Share. Marvel at how amazing the world around me can be. To not ignore all the things that are wrong in our towns, cities, states, and country. To not ignore the terrible things that you read about every day in the newspaper. But before solving the world's problems, to focus on those people around you that you love most. Your family. Your tribe. It sounds easy and it should be. Because outside of finding yourself, building a family is the most elemental thing that makes us human. Gives us purpose in life.

For the first time in years, I didn't feel alone. I felt full inside. It was a great feeling. One I promised myself I would never let go of again.

CHAPTER 7

Friends: Less Is More: The Unbalanced Friend Portfolio Theory

Quitting drinking was one of the hardest things I ever did. Not because I had an alcohol addiction. Like I previously mentioned, I drank to curb social anxiety, to use it as a social lubricant to become what I thought was my best self. To be witty. Funny. Fun. And because my best friend since my twenties loved to drink. And boy could he drink. Ten martinis in a night. No problem. Cocktails all night and then run at six in the morning. I was convinced that my best friend had a different type of blood running through veins. One that got stronger, not weaker, the more he drank. His ancestors were from Northern Europe. The place where vodka was created. I imagined that my friend was like the biblical character Sampson who, when he got his hair cut off, lost all his strength. As hair was to Sampson, vodka was to my friend Matt.

When I told him at age thirty-nine that Vanessa and I were separating, he was beyond supportive. Did more than a good friend was supposed to do. He let me sleep in his living room for two months while Vanessa and I worked things out. However, the one thing he couldn't accept was when I told him that I was stopping drinking. Or at least stopping 90-plus percent of my former consumption.

Matt was from Cleveland, and in Cleveland men drank. That's what they did. That's how they bonded. Same with my friend Rom, who was also from Cleveland. To tell these guys that I was giving up drinking, that I was happy to go out with them but that I'd have a Perrier while they were drinking martinis, basically vodka straight-up, insulted their machismo. Their way of doing things. It just wasn't done in our circle of friends.

However, the doctor had scared me with the warning that if I didn't change my life, I might not live past fifty. So, I did what I'd always done in my life when confronted by a hard decision. Initially, I ignored it. I went back out with Matt. We got super drunk together. I shamelessly hit on women even though my divorce was fresh and I didn't want to meet anyone. I just wanted to center myself. I showed off to Matt and Rom how much I could drink. If they wanted to drink five martinis in a night, I would drink ten.

This phase, luckily, didn't last long. Since I had my goal of eating healthy. Living healthy. Exercising every morning. Running. Surfing. Feeling good inside was so addictive that I realized that the drinking had to go. Matt and Rom either had to accept the new me, or I'd have to find new friends. I didn't come right out and say that to them, since I was too scared to do that. Instead, I just slowly faded away. When Matt would ask me if I could go out, I'd make an excuse. I was busy working on an analysis for Chad or Steve, when nothing could be farther from the truth, since, as I've previously mentioned, I had all my work done for them each week by Tuesday. On the weekends, I was off surfing every morning and, in the evenings, before I met Christina, I filled them with dating a whole assortment of different women. While this wasn't good for my wallet and it got super-tiring fast, it kept me from going out drinking every night with the guys.

And then one day it happened. Matt and I were sitting at a bar, and he ordered a vodka soda. I ordered a water. He said right then and there that he couldn't continue to hang out with me if I didn't drink with him. He couldn't drink if I didn't drink. Those were the rules. I was terrified inside. Matt had been my best friend since I was twenty-one. Since we had started working together at McKinsey & Company. He'd been a few years my senior when I'd gotten to the consulting firm straight out of Pomona College.

I still remember my first day of when I showed up and was surrounded by all these great-looking guys that were all easily over six feet tall. And all the women dressed attractively in power suits. While I had on a nice suit as well, I felt uncomfortable in it. It didn't help that I'd spent all summer between college and starting work at McKinsey out drinking every night and windsurfing and running outside during the day. My face was overly tan and used to the sun. Now trapped inside fancy consulting offices, my face was starting to ooze with grease, since there was no natural sunlight to dry it out. I was also sweating profusely, creating huge dark circles under my armpits. To make matters even worse, I'd never worn a tie before, except at a few weddings, and I'd tied the one I was wearing way too tight. It felt like it was cutting off my ability to breathe. Which it was. However, I didn't dare untie it since everyone else had their ties perfectly cinched tight. Only years later would I learn the secret that the way to have your tie cinched tight and not strangle yourself was to buy your shirts with a collar a half size too big. But at the time, I didn't know that and thought, how in the world am I going to last working for two years—the length of the McKinsey analyst program—not being able to breathe?

Right when I was feeling the most flummoxed, in walked Matt. He looked totally different from everyone else. Like me, he was overly tan. What I would later learn was that he loved to sail, lived on a sailboat, and spent his weekends sailing off the coast of Marina Del Rey, where he lived. He had blonde hair that he wore long, particularly in front. His hair was cut as though someone had put a bowl on his head and just cut around it. His hair in the front was so long that he looked like a sheep dog. You couldn't see Matt's eyes, and I wondered how he could see anything. Even more, I wondered how he'd ended up at McKinsey, since he seemed so different from everyone else. I found out quickly. Because he was wicked smart. A highly intuitive and analytic thinker. He was one of the prized analysts on the team, because he needed almost no sleep, he had a brilliant, creative, problem-solving mind, and the clients loved him.

I decided then and there, at the age of twenty-one, even before I'd spoken a word to Matt, that he was going to be my new best friend. I invited him to go see a movie in Santa Monica, and afterward we'd hunted to find my car. There are eight garages in Santa Monica that all look identical, and it took us over four hours to find where we'd parked. While we looked entirely different on the outside—me buffed, over six feet tall, and dressed like a preppy guy while Matt was shorter, slim, and dressed casually like a surfer crossed with a *Star*

Trek geek—inside we shared a lot in common. First off, as the garage incident taught us, we were both super absent-minded professor types. Lost in our heads versus in the world that was around us. Second, we both loved a good adventure. I thought it was so cool that Matt lived on a boat, drove an old 1970s yellow Targa Porsche, painted on the weekends, and still managed to work at one of the best consulting companies during the week.

I secretly confided in him that I was totally stressed out. That I felt like I was doing a terrible job at McKinsey. While I had studied economics in college, I had no idea how businesses really worked. I didn't know anything about accounting. How profit and loss statements, cash flow statements, and balance sheets all tied together. I'd spent an entire week building one slide out of the twenty slides assigned to me by my boss, and she'd almost flipped out. She'd looked at me apoplectically and asked how in the world I thought it was okay to show up after five days of work with only 5 percent of it done. I'd sheepishly told her that it had taken me that long to find the data. I'd made endless calls to multiple companies, I'd gone to multiple libraries and read multiple books and articles to get all the data needed to fill that one slide. And boy, I thought to myself, did it look good. She'd then told me something that I've never forgotten, that it was the essence of the slide's story that mattered, not getting each and every data point that lay behind it. I could have told the same story that slide was meant to tell with a whole range of data. Simply put, she said, if I was going to survive at McKinsey, I was going to have to work much faster. To the tune of 20X since I'd only gotten one out of twenty slides done in time for her.

As I sat on Matt's boat drinking the wine he'd poured for the two of us, Matt turned on some Brazilian bossa nova music. He loved the song "The Girl from Ipanema" and played it over and over. Looking back, we were both trying too hard to be cool. To be rebels against the boring business suits we wore by day. But at the same, I thought that Matt was the coolest guy in the world. And he had some simple advice for me. I was sleeping too much. What? That sounded crazy. No, he told me that the reason that I was so stressed out was that I was sleeping so much that I was overly clear during the day. It was making me realize everything that I was doing wrong. It was overwhelming my brain with too much business stimuli. No, the way to get better, as he poured me another glass of wine, was to sleep less. To stay up all night having fun. Drinking wine. Not having a care in the world. I'd be so groggy in the morning that there was no way I could be stressed, Matt reasoned. And when I wasn't stressed, the work would go great.

Matt's sleep deprivation idea seemed totally crazy, but as I was getting more stressed by the day, I was desperate to try anything. Strangely enough it worked. I went from eight hours to seven hours to six hours down to five and eventually to four hours a night. With all this newfound time on my hands, Matt and I went out late nights and prowled LA. We'd drive from the beach all the way to downtown on the infamous Sunset Strip. We'd go to cool after-hours clubs Matt knew about in LA's abandoned warehouses, and then we'd drive back toward the beach town where we lived. Our goal, especially on the weekends, was to stay awake all night, since our favorite breakfast spot offered 50 percent off omelets if you arrived there at 6: 00 A.M.

Flash forward, and now I was sitting on a bar stool next to my best buddy for the past twenty years, and he'd laid down the gauntlet. If I didn't want to drink with him anymore, he wasn't sure he could be friends with me. It was a crushing blow. I was even more devastated since I had just gotten divorced from Vanessa and for the first time in eight years was sleeping alone every night. My apartment felt empty. Some nights I'd just sit on the couch and marvel at how quiet everything was around me. That if I died, who would know? Who would come looking for me? And now my best friend, the guy that I'd grown up idolizing, had put a stark choice before me. Continue my partying ways with him or go in separate directions.

My analytic brain went into overdrive. What were the pros and cons of staying friends with Matt? The obvious pro was that he meant everything to me. The obvious con was that drinking every night was destroying my life. My well-being. Visiting the doctor had been my life wake-up call. I realized that there was nothing, no matter how much it hurt, that could separate me from taking care of myself. Of saying I was done. I told Matt he was my best friend, but I had to go. I got up and left.

The next weeks were hard. I had a new friend that I've mentioned named Ian, whom I surfed with each morning. I had a cool new job working for Chad and Steve at their start-up that I'd sold my last company to. I started dating Christina, and things in my life all seemed good. The hole in my life was my friends. I missed Matt. I missed Rom. I missed their camaraderie. I knew that I could not go back to who I was before, but I also didn't want to lose the lifelong friendships of two of my best buddies.

Like many things in my life, the answer came to me one day when I was least expecting it. I was fiddling around, adjusting the stocks in my portfolio one day. I realized that I had too many stocks that I didn't know anything about. That I didn't care about. I started to sell the stocks one after another. Big blue-chip boring CPG company I didn't care about. Sold. Big oil company that went against my morals no matter how profitable it was. Sold. Big media company that made movies I didn't like. Sold. I kept culling and culling until at the end I only had a few stocks left that I loved. That I treasured. That I wasn't going to sell for any reason. Because they were good companies. Sure, they had their ups and downs like any other company, but they had great fundamentals. Solid business models. Were in exciting spaces, mainly technology, that I loved and knew something about.

And then that's when it hit me that great friends were like great companies. The key wasn't having a ton of them, but only a few of them that you over-invested in. The corollary was that there were a bunch of other ones that you should under-invest in. To divest your friend portfolio of everyone who wasn't essential. To have an unbalanced portfolio of only your closest and best friends.

By this time, I'd stopped working for Chad and Steve and started a new company called Lasso. It was a real-time wine and cheese delivery service, basically a party in a box. It felt incongruous to me that I was fixated on being healthy at the same time that I had started a business that was all about delivering booze all over the country as fast as possible. But like many things in my life, when I didn't synch my analytic and intuitive sides of my brain together, I often ended up making poor decisions. More on Lasso and why it didn't work later . . .

For now, the important point was that I was back to working seventy to eighty hours a week again. To being foolishly brave. Doing another start-up even though I'd just turned forty. And I simply didn't have time for tons of friends. And I desperately missed my friendships with Matt, Rom, and my best buddy from college that I'd kind of lost touch with, Praveen. I decided even though Matt and Rom loved to drink and I had to stop, there was no way in the world I was going to stop being friends with them. Things just had to change.

I met with Matt and told him he was my best friend, that I loved him like a brother, and whether he liked it or not, he was my best friend. I told him that, while I might have an occasional drink with him, I wasn't going to go booze it up every night, and he needed to learn to deal with it. To grow up. To stop pouting over something as simple as Midwest drinking matters. So what if he drank and I didn't? So what if I drank Perrier and he drank vodka? I let him know that I could still be ten times crazier and more fun than he was, even if I was stone-cold sober.

Because that was the dirty secret. All these years that I'd been getting sloshed, I had thought it was the booze that made me funny. Crazy. Weird. Cool. The life of the party. While it had lowered my inhibitions, it had actually just dulled me. When I started to go out with Matt sober, I was actually funnier. More alert. More alive. Now it was my choice if I jumped up on the bar and yelled something stupid. I had even more energy and could stay out all night whenever I wanted.

I also reconnected with my friend Praveen. He was my best friend in college. Like me, he had grown overweight after too many years of hard partying. I challenged him to a weight loss competition. Praveen, being supercompetitive like me, lost a bunch of weight. He looked great. He felt great. I was proud even though I never said anything to Praveen that I'd had a good impact on his life, since he'd had a great impact on mine, especially when I was going through tough times in college.

Rom was a different story. He was a guy's guy through and through. He didn't want to talk about feelings. He would never relate, as Matt finally did, that it was okay for me not to drink as much. But Rom was and is a fiercely loyal friend. He is the guy who we've always joked that we'd call if we needed to bury a body in the middle of the night that we'd call Rom. We wouldn't call Matt, because he's a lawyer by training. Matt would ask all sorts of questions about who the person was. Whether an illegal act had been committed. Of course it had, or why would you be calling him in the middle of the night to bury the body? So Matt was definitely out. Praveen was just cautious by nature. He, like Rom, was a fiercely loyal guy, but there was no way in a million years I could imagine Praveen taking out a shovel and helping to bury a body. Which is a good thing. Because Praveen is a great guy.

Rom was different. Not because he was a bad person. Just because, like me, he was a serial entrepreneur. He loved to take risks. The bigger the better. He wasn't born rich, and everything Rom had he'd made for himself. He supported his mother. He supported his brothers and sisters. While Rom's morals may have been a bit looser than the other three guys in the group, he was every bit the most loyal, most stand-up guy who you could count on 1000 percent.

So, when I told Rom that I wasn't going to drink as much anymore. He didn't accept it the way Matt did. We didn't talk about the reasons why. About how my divorce from Vanessa had been devastating. How the doctor had scared the bejesus out of me. How at 50 pounds overweight I'd been really depressed. Like I said, Rom is a guy's guy. That kind of talk was for wussies. And that's all Rom said. If I wanted to not drink, then I was a wuss. Period. No further discussion. However, I could tell from the smile on his face as he said it that we'd still be best friends. Just different now. He and Matt as the machismo men who could slay dragons with the amount they drank. Me as the wussy who sipped Perrier beside them.

Having my friends back was a great feeling. While your family is your inner tribe. Your best friends are your outer tribe. They are the ones who connect you to the greater world around you. Make you feel wanted. Needed in the world. Let you see the world from a completely different lens than your own. They are also a critical part of your own narrative, since they've known you since you were young. They create a through line of continuing as the world changes around you.

I decided that from this moment on, I would over-invest in my three best friends. One of them was getting married anywhere in the world? I was there. One of them needed help? A loan? I was there. One of them said they wanted to stay out to all hours of the night? Count me in (minus the drinking part). I'd reconstituted my friendship group, and it felt great.

And then I added one more guy to the mix. His name was Tyler. He was 6'3", had bright red hair, and looked like a sun god. He'd won *The Amazing Race* years before, he was a local celebrity in San Francisco, and one of the craziest, zaniest people you'd ever met in your life. He was also the most positive person I've ever met. He literally radiated life. And positivity was what I needed, because my start-up Lasso had run out of money, my VCs were pissed that I'd lost all their dough, my bank account was dropping fast because I'd stopped paying myself a salary, and my buddies Matt, Rom, and Praveen were all off doing fabulously well.

I had a new idea that I hadn't told anyone about yet. Not even Christina. And I knew just the man I wanted to go talk to about it. His name was Tyler. It was a single conversation at his restaurant that would forever change the direction of the next chapter of my life.

CHAPTER 8

Business: The Entrepreneur's Dilemma: The $100M Business Model

"10,000 customers is 100 million dollars in business."

I stared across the table at Tyler's restaurant, West of Pecos, as I said that. I waited for him to reply. In an instant, Tyler smiled and said that he was in. Later, we would both learn that the new idea I had would take about fifty thousand users per $100 million, so I was off by 5X of my initial statement. However, even that was a ridiculously good ratio compared to the earlier businesses that I'd built, including the mobile social network where we'd had millions of users and each month made little more than zero.

I'd known Tyler MacNiven for over ten years. He was a friend of my good friend Chris who'd created the crazy online pants company called Betabrand. The same pants company that made the Discorounds that we'd all been wearing when I met Christina. Tyler, or Tee as I liked to call him, was a local legend in San Francisco. He'd won *The Amazing Race* a bunch of years before with his friend BJ. They were called "The Hippies," and they'd dusted all the great-looking, buffed, all-American types the season they were on the show. By being smarter. More resourceful. Friendly. Funny.

Tee had done really cool things after *The Amazing Race*. He'd walked the length of Japan and made a film about it. He'd created another film called *Wrestling Mongolia*. I'd gotten to know him when I ran Zannel, and we did this funny idea that was ahead of its time in 2005 called *9 to 5*. The idea had come from my friend Chris, the CEO of Betabrand. Chris thought that the coolest thing about Zannel was that it showed your life in real time. Why not put the technology to use by following a person's day from nine to five with instant updates every hour on the hour? It was a simple idea that was all about who you were following, but I said sure since Chris always dressed up any idea with the most zany, funny guys he was friends with. And this time proved no different. He called me and said that his friend Tyler was in for the *9 to 5* show, and they had the perfect bit for it. They needed our mobile film crew to head over to the Mission where Tyler was sitting in an easy chair.

For Tyler's *9 to 5* show, his idea was that he would rely on the kindness of strangers to push him in the easy chair across the entire city of San Francisco—from the Mission to San Francisco's most recognized icon, the Golden Gate Bridge. Tyler would tell the audience stories along the way, pee in a cup since he couldn't get out of a chair, and chat with the tourists. In Japanese. Spanish. German. I was astounded how many people this long-haired, wild-eyed, self-described hippy spoke to. And it was riveting TV. Tyler was by turns funny. Bizarre. Shameless. Unafraid of the camera. Quite the contrary—when the camera was on, he was magnetic. Like gravity. Pulling all of us toward him. I was laughing my ass off as a group of Japanese tourists pushed him the final leg of the tour to the Golden Gate Bridge. While they snapped photos with him, Tyler asked them in Japanese what they'd had for breakfast, and he then asked another one if they'd mind emptying out his pee bottle so he could refill it. He said it so normally and friendly that the young tourist man said sure in Japanese and went off to do it.

Flash forward ten years later, and Tee and I were sitting across from each other at his restaurant. He'd had a good run since riding on the easy chair across the city. Like I said, he'd made a few funny movies. He and his brothers, who also were tall and extremely good-looking, had dated some of San Francisco's coolest girls. And he'd created with his brothers a bunch of successful themed restaurants. In San Francisco, he and his brothers were regarded as restaurant royalty. Particularly because their father, Jamis, had started one of the most iconic restaurants in the Bay Area called Buck's. Buck's was a mid-sized diner down in the heart of Silicon Valley in a small town called Woodside. Close to Silicon Valley's famed Sand Hill Road, Buck's had been the spot where many famed Silicon Valley deals were consummated. Jamis liked to tell the story of how the original founder of Tesla, the guy who created one of the first electric cars before Elon Musk got involved, used to eat at Buck's all the time. How he'd offered Jamis an ability to invest in his electric car company. How Jamis, who viewed himself as a futurist, hadn't seen the future on this one and had declined.

Buck's was one of those amazing California establishments that was just cool. It featured photos all over the walls of all the adventures Jamis had gone on when he was young. It also had hanging all of the strange, random things Jamis had bought at flea markets from all over the world. It had Jamis's groovy artwork on the walls and sculptures sitting beside tables. Jamis was the original legend of the MacNiven clan, and Tyler and his brothers wanted to be just like him. It was only later that I would learn that it was Mrs. MacNiven, Jamis's wife, who was the brilliant one. The woman behind the guy who made Jamis's entire zany world possible.

But back to Tyler and me. We'd kept in touch periodically over the years. However, not too much because we were both running our businesses. And frankly, because Tyler and his gang were much cooler than me. Anyway, flash back to the present and my idea. It was a big idea that had hit me right as Lasso, my wine and cheese delivery start-up, a not-so-big idea, was going down the tubes. Did people want booze delivered to their home? Sure. Would they love some cheese with that? Of course? Was the combo of those two items inherently a bad business model? No. Was how I executed it terrible? Absolutely yes.

I'd started Lasso after I left Chad and Steve's start-up. Nothing had gone as planned with the famous Internet founders. Sure, they had been stand-up guys and they'd paid Braxton, me, and the other guys to join them handsomely as part of buying our business. But to put it simply, the gods of luck didn't shine down on them this time. They'd had such a run of hits it was incredible. Both Chad and Steve had been some of the first employees at PayPal. Steve had gone on to work as one of the first coders at Facebook. They'd started YouTube at first to be a video dating site. Then at the last minute they'd had the idea to make it a way bigger idea. Why not just make it a video sharing site? Since there was no good way to share homemade videos on the web at the time. And the sites that had done it were too slow. Had crappy content. Basically stunk.

YouTube was and is one of the all-time great Internet sensation stories. Unlike most Silicon Valley start-ups where you have to try multiple different ideas before one of them sticks, YouTube from the moment it started was a viral hit. Users flocked to the site. YouTube videos spread fast and furiously across the net, and people clicked the "Share" button thousands of times. Then millions of times. Then billions of times. Chad and Steve confided in me that the reason they sold YouTube to Google was that the video sharing site was growing too fast. Their main investor, Sequoia Capital, was convinced that unless Google, which had built an incredible tech backbone to handle YouTube's type of video search and play volume, acquired the company, that YouTube was on the verge of blowing up.

For a guy that had spent his entire adult like trying to create a hit and getting close but never quite there, that was a mind-blowing thing to think about. A service growing too fast. Out of control. It fit with the paradigm that Bill Gurley, one of Silicon Valley's best VCs, once told me when I pitched him Zannel. I had carefully constructed a growth curve on a slide that showed that Zannel would grow nicely but not wildly over time. Bill stopped me mid-sentence and told me that my model was all wrong. As I attempted to explain to him that I was an ex-McKinsey analyst, he cut me off again. Frankly, it had nothing to do with highfalutin assumptions. Either your online consumer company took off like a rocket ship or it didn't. If it did, VCs would pour rocket fuel, code language in VC speak for investing in your company, to make it grow even faster. If it didn't, VCs likely wouldn't give you a dime, and your company, likely without a real business model, would go bust.

However, the gods of luck had not shone down on Chad and Steve's new company called AVOS. And they hadn't necessarily done anything wrong. They'd hired a bunch of crackerjack engineers by buying my company, and they'd acquired del.icio.us, one of Silicon Valley's most beloved sites, which they wanted to resuscitate with the Chad and Steve magic. However, a lot had changed since they launched YouTube. Online users were fickle. They'd love one site and hate the next. And while some new users loved the relaunched del.icio.us we built, the core users hated it. Not because anything we'd done was bad, but because it was different. A great learning lesson that sometimes it's better to start fresh than to try to fix a broken site, no matter how noble the intentions.

After six months of del.icio.us flatlining, I'd left to go start something new. Not because I didn't like Chad or Steve. Or because I didn't think they were brilliant. Or didn't believe in their long-term vision. Quite the contrary. It was because I had literally nothing to do. Without the rebuilt del.icio.us zooming up into the sky of millions of users, there wasn't anything for me to do on the business development side. Chad knew and I knew that I had the entrepreneurial bug still coursing through my veins. He gave me a hug and wished me well.

So, at the age of forty or forty-one, I can't remember which, I started my new start-up Lasso. I didn't give much thought to the business model or how I'd grow the user base. I just thought it would be cool to do something local. Create an app where I could press a button and things would be brought to me. I knew just the engineer I wanted to work with again. Braxton. Who'd left AVOS right around the time I did, since they also didn't need a CTO for a site that wasn't experiencing rocket ship growth. Braxton was really bummed that the thing with Chad and Steve hadn't worked out. They were his heroes, and he figured that it was just his bad luck that the one time they finally didn't have a hit, he'd been at that one instead of their prior glorious companies. I gently reminded Braxton that he, unlike me, had already had a hit with the mobile ringtone company. I was still searching for my first one.

Unlike with Zannel, we decided that we were going to go small team this time with Lasso. It was one of the great lessons we learned at the feet of Chad and Steve. Watching how they built a start-up up close. They favored small teams. Full-stack engineers. As part of working with Steve, Braxton had taught himself to code again. It was Steve's belief that everyone on the engineering team, even the CTO, had to be a coder, and this included Braxton. As I've mentioned, Braxton is one of the smartest guys I've ever known, and in no time his fingers were flying across the keyboard again. This time building Lasso's platform himself versus hiring a bunch of other engineers to do it for him. We added one more guy to the mix. An incredible app developer named James who loves to drink whiskey late into the night. He thought a wine and cheese app was a great idea. He was in.

It was easy for Braxton and me to raise money for Lasso. Unlike most industries where failure is viewed as a bad thing, in Silicon Valley it's viewed as a badge of honor. The fact that the thing with Chad and Steve hadn't worked out didn't matter. VCs looked at that as though it was more experience, more data points for entrepreneurs to learn from so that when they did their next start-up, they would do it even better. Our main investor, Tim, later confided in me that he loved to back guys who'd had a recent stinging loss, since it made them hungrier, made them have, to use his expression, "their hair on fire." He was also a bit superstitious. He believed that eventually lightning would strike us, since Braxton and I were hardworking and, he reasoned, due for a hit.

While money was easy to raise, what Braxton and I had not expected was how hard it would be to start again from the ground up. To be working for peanuts when we were over the age of forty. Especially when we both had friends who were now making over $1 million a year as lawyers, Google execs, bankers—anything but us. Not that money meant everything to Braxton and me, but it did matter. For simple things. Christina would invite me to go with her to Mexico to go to one of her friend's weddings. I would say that I had too much work to do and that would create a fight between us. But the reality was that I was worried about spending too much money and didn't want to admit that to her. It wasn't that I didn't have money in my bank account, because I did from the Zannel and Tap11 sales; it was that when you are making almost nothing, your natural inclination is to not want to spend. Eat into your principal. It makes you think small versus big.

And Lasso, despite all our enthusiasm, turned out to be a small idea. We had the right idea to focus on a single-use case. Our previous start-ups had taught us that lesson. However, wine and cheese delivery in one city ordered on your mobile phone turned out to be too narrow. Like I said, it was an awesome experience for users but a terrible business model. For multiple reasons. It was superexpensive to advertise on

Facebook, the primary means to acquire users at the time, in one hyper-local place (and especially San Francisco, ground zero for almost all start-ups) versus advertising broadly across the country if your app was not location specific. It was super hard to scale our wine and cheese idea since we relied on local wine and cheese stores for inventory. While I love a customer going to amazing, local artisan stores, partnering with them was a disaster. Not because the local proprietors weren't great people. Quite the contrary. They were awesome. It was because they weren't making any money. The toll that big box retailers and online giants like Amazon had on them was much harder than I originally realized. They cut their prices so much, particularly the wine stores, that there wasn't much money left for a partnership with us. The best partnership we created gave us 10 percent of the sales, and this is where our business model spectacularly failed.

Like any start-up that's 110 percent focused on customers, we offered free shipping and the same price as in-store. Great for consumers, but again, terrible for us as a business that was quickly running out of money. The math was simple. It cost us $40 to acquire a customer on Facebook. The average order size on Lasso was $40—a bottle of wine and a few knick-knacks from the cheese store. We made 10 percent of $40, which was $4. So, it worked as long as we got more than 10 orders, right? But on average we only got 5 orders, which turned our business model upside down: $20 per customer in revenues minus $40 to acquire that customer meant we lost $20. But it didn't stop there. Each free delivery cost us $5, so we ended up down $45 per customer. At the same time, we were paying expensive engineers to continue to add more and more features. Within two years of starting Lasso, we'd gone through the roughly $2 million we'd raised. I went to Sand Hill

Road to raise more money, and the feedback was consistent. The VCs loved the idea of the app and said they would all use it for their next party. However, they all immediately saw that the unit economics were terrible. They asked the obvious questions. Had we considered charging a shipping fee? Yes, but the competition didn't. Had we considered raising prices above the store price? Yes, but technically we weren't supposed to because under California law we were a marketplace, not a licensed liquor merchant, and had to pass on the retail price versus set a new one for the customer. After getting numerous no's from a bunch of VCs, I asked one what they were investing in, since he clearly wasn't going to invest in me. He started to gush about how amazing the food delivery apps were. People were literally ordering every week. Week after week. The stickiness of these apps was amazing. He had to go because he was about to meet the founder of one of the best ones.

I went home depressed that I'd created an app that had a terrible business model that no one wanted to fund. That I hadn't been clever enough to focus on food and instead had focused on a cool use case, but one that was too infrequent to support a wide adoption business model. I moped about my apartment for a few weeks. I got into a big fight with Braxton, who by this point was also souring on the fact that Lasso wasn't working. He was burnt out after Chad and Steve's thing not working and now Lasso looking like it was headed for the dustbin. At my lowest point, I'm embarrassed to say, on Christina's birthday I showed up six hours late to pick her up to go on her special birthday weekend that I'd arranged. Because I was upset. Because I was disorganized. Because I'd woken up late. Focusing more on myself than on the fact that it was her special day. Worse, I'd been testy in the car all the way to Yosemite. At one point, Christina had been so annoyed she'd said that if I didn't be quiet, she wanted me to immediately pull over and she'd get an Uber and go back home. I'd reassured her that I'd clean up my act so we could have a good weekend. But I couldn't get the feeling of failure out of my head. At my lowest point of the weekend, while we were hiking up one of Yosemite's gloriously beautiful trails, I'd sat down in the middle of the trail and told Christina that I couldn't keep going. I was done.

"You're done?" she'd asked incredulously. "Done with what?" With everything I said overdramatically. I was feeling really sorry for myself. Like the universe was conspiring against me. That no matter what I did, it wasn't working. I was conveniently forgetting that this same universe had been around when I sold my company to the YouTube founders, lost 50 pounds, and met Christina by chance at a bar neither of us ever went to. But at this moment all I could think about was how unlucky I was. Christina, never one to dwell on too much negativity, said that if I wanted to sit in the middle of the trail, that was my choice. She was going to enjoy her birthday hiking up the trail and she'd see me later. And she left. And I sat there. For a long time. Feeling foolish. Feeling alone again. Feeling like an idiot that had just let the one thing that was really positive in my life disappear around the bend.

And then like many times in my life when I least expected it, a simple idea popped into my head. If food apps were working, why didn't I start one? Who cares if I didn't create the first one? Most of my problems as an entrepreneur had been that I was always too early. Zannel was the mobile media sharing app before powerful phones like the iPhone existed to support fast, large file transfer. Tap11 was the real-time mobile media sharing and analytics platform before big enterprise firms had allocated a budget to spend on such an item. Both ideas turned out to be prescient—Instagram became a viral sensation years after we stopped working on Zannel and sold to Facebook for a billion dollars, and social media measurement platforms became highly valuable as social advertising became the #1 way to grow user bases online. Further, I loved food. While maybe I wasn't a foodie, I'd grown up cooking. I'd taken cooking classes as a kid. I'd read *Joy of Cooking* as a nine-year-old and taught myself how to make Caesar salad. Chinese egg rolls. Moo Shu Pork. I was by no means a gourmet cook, but I knew how to make all my restaurant favorites. More importantly, I had just lost 50 pounds by eating healthy and changing my diet. And that was going to be my edge. My thing that was different. All the food apps were focused on eating indulgent, greasy restaurant food. Pizza. Burgers. Fried chicken. My app was going to be about only delivering healthy food.

I chased after Christina excitedly to tell her that I had a new idea. She justifiably was pissed for me not making her birthday weekend all about her. But she knew how obsessed I got about new ideas, so she patiently and sweetly listened to it as we hiked up the trail. When I was done, there was a long pause before she said anything. Then finally, as I stared out at the great expanse beneath us, Christina said simply that it was a great idea. Was it better than Lasso, I asked? "Yes," she said. "Now please be quiet, so we can enjoy the rest of our weekend." And I did the right thing. From that moment on, I focused on her. We finished a great hike. Then went out for a great dinner. I was my best self, as inside I felt giddy with excitement again. As an entrepreneur, only two things sustain you. When your start-up is growing like crazy. Or when you have an exciting new idea.

There was only one problem. I didn't know the first thing about creating a food company. Which is why I went to see Tyler, whose family had created one hit restaurant after another. However, before I went, I did something I'd never done before when starting a new idea. I built a business model. I know what you may be thinking. *Well that's obvious.* Who would ever start a company without a business model? And especially me, because I'd worked at McKinsey. No, what I mean is that I built a real business model that I believed in. That the assumptions were grounded in reality. With all my prior businesses, I'd built business models for Zannel, Tap11, Lasso, and even for del.icio.us that were grounded in wishful thinking: Well, if this great thing happens and then this great thing happens and then that one, then wouldn't it be great. The start-up will be a success. Assumptions like I could acquire all my users for free. Or that they would use the app every day because I wanted it to be that way, not because it was grounded in any insight.

No, with my new healthy food start-up I was going to do it the old-fashioned way. Intuition had popped the great idea into my head. However, I was going to use hardcore logic to build my business model one assumption at a time. Each assumption would intentionally be conservative. More importantly, I would make a simple business model that showed in ten rows of an Excel spreadsheet what needed to happen for the business to reach $100 million in annual revenue run rate (AAR).

Why $100 million? Because that's the magic number that venture capitalists will tell you allows you to become a public company. To be taken seriously as a real company. And as a guy who desperately wanted to move beyond all the hype of "playing" Silicon Valley CEO to becoming what I viewed as a real one, if $100 million in revenue was what it took, then I'd center all the energy in my business model on how to reach that. The funny thing when you talk to most beginning entrepreneurs that while they think too aspirationally about how many cool features their app will have, what I like to call "first-time entrepreneur featuritis," very few think big enough about their business model. The adage in Silicon Valley is if you create a cool product, then you'll find your way to a great business model. While that works as long as you have millions of users, I wanted to build an online model where with thousands of users you could build a really big business.

So, I did the hard, unsexy work of building my $100 million business model for my new healthy food company, for which I still didn't have a name. The first model had all the key assumptions in it. A realistic price to acquire each customer, what we call in Silicon Valley CAC (customer acquisition cost), the average price each customer would pay for my healthy box of food, or what we call AOV (average order value), how often each customer would order my healthy food box, or what I identified in the model as my purchase rate, and finally what margin I would make on each box of food based on my cost of goods sold. I tried to ground each assumption based on actual data of what other companies had experienced. When I was done, I was shocked to see that it appeared that ten thousand users equaled a $100 million business. No wonder I thought that the VCs were rushing in to invest in food apps. It seemed too good to be true. But I checked and then rechecked my model. Just for fun, I did a simple version of my Lasso model, and it showed that I'd need at least two million users to get to a $100 million business. Without knowing it at the time, I'd just learned the most valuable lesson I'd ever gotten in business. It was a dead simple one. Know your business model. Inside and out. Prove to yourself that it will work before you sell it to others. Construct a simple narrative in your mind and on paper of how you can reach $100 million business without any crazy assumptions. Without having to have a viral hit. Without lightning having to strike you on the head. I've advised now over a dozen entrepreneurs and as simple as that lesson is, you'd be surprised that not one had built a $100 million model. Many product-focused entrepreneurs hadn't built a model at all, or if they had, they'd had their finance guy do it. Or they'd created a model to show VCs something that looked good but wasn't grounded in any facts. I stopped each and every one of them from telling me about their product. That could come later. First, they needed to build their $100 million model themselves. In a room by themselves. Only moving forward with their idea after they didn't break it on the white board. Since it's a lot easier to kill an idea before you've raised venture capital and hired a bunch of engineers than after you're neck deep. It's the most benevolent thing you can do for your team, because it will mean that you're starting on solid footing. Even though you'll be wrong.

You'll be wrong, like I was, because inevitably you didn't get everything right in your model. There were things you left out. However, even if you are off the mark somewhat, the fact that you know the four or five key variables that make your business work means that you can do the next most important thing that great serial entrepreneurs do: hire a great team. And I knew just who I wanted for my food start-up, as I've previously mentioned, Tyler, from the restaurant royalty family of the MacNivens.

Unlike ideas that I'd pitched Tyler over the years that he'd said no to, most notably to Lasso, Tyler immediately said yes to the healthy food idea. He loved that ten thousand users equaled $100 million business, since we'd both seen how hard it was to generate millions of users and ten thousand didn't seem like that much. (Even later when it turned out to be fifty thousand, that was still way less than millions). More importantly, I learned another super-important lesson right then and there. The importance of a company's mission. Having grown up on a farm, Tyler loved the fact that we were going to focus on healthy food. Making people's lives better. What they teach in business schools are social impact businesses. Businesses with a double bottom line.

He loved the sustainability aspect of our company. Where up to 50 percent of food is normally thrown away, with our company we would ship you the freshest pre-measured ingredients plus recipes so there would be no waste. He wasn't crazy about the amount of packaging it would take to ship the box, but I assured him we'd do everything in our power to make our boxes the most sustainable they could be. And we did. We came up with the first 100 percent recyclable and compostable box. Even today, millions of boxes shipped later, we're working on our next version to make our box even more sustainable, since that's one of the values Tyler holds most dear. I loved the idea, too. Right after I'd started Lasso, which was basically a glorified booze delivery service under the guise of being a wine and cheese delivery service, I'd felt uncomfortable. I went back to my old adage, while many things are difficult, few are worth doing. And sending people every week the healthiest, most delicious food that could help make their families healthier felt absolutely great, like just the right the thing to do.

Joining in the journey with Tyler and me was George, one of my oldest friends and co-company creators, who is a marvelous human being and a truly creative soul. Together, he and Tyler would work on the creative part of the business while I went back to my VCs and bank investors and convinced them to allow me to pivot Lasso to the new healthy food company. Alas, Braxton, while he was super supportive of the new idea and thought it was one of my best yet, told me it was time to get off the start-up train. He needed a break. A life reset. He was going to go become the CTO of one of LA's largest media companies. He'd stay on to help get the new platform up and running and then stay on the board if that was okay. Braxton's analogy was that we were two alpha males that had been trapped in a closet for multiple years, the closet represented the small start-ups we'd created together. It was time for him to step out of the closet. Get some fresh air. Allow me to stay there and have some space. Do what I thought was right versus second-guessing each other. Work with some new fresh faces. Like Tyler, whom we both agreed had the amazing good energy the new idea needed. Our app developer, James, luckily did stay on board. But he moved to Washington State where he'd always wanted to live.

I thought we were set to go, but Tyler said it was critical that we hire one more person. A chef. Of course we needed to do that. But as obvious as that sounds, I'd always done the product myself. Which is how you create a good product, but not a great one if you don't happen to be as talented as Apple's Jonathan Ive. So, we went searching for our chef. It was great fun as we had the chefs come to Tyler's kitchen and cook for Tyler, George, and me. We paid them fairly for the evening, and we had some stunning meals. However, despite how good these chefs were, they weren't right for our company. Many didn't want to cook healthy food. Having grown up in the restaurant business, they'd learned to make food taste delicious by adding three key ingredients: salt, butter, and sugar. Three of the key things I'd just avoided when I lost 50 pounds. Right as I felt like giving up on our search, I received an email from the head of one of San Francisco's best restaurants, The Slanted Door. A Vietnamese restaurant that had just won the James Beard Award for being one of the best restaurants in the United States. Her name was Justine Kelly, and from the moment I met her, I knew that my luck had radically just changed. She was a single working mom who had spent her entire career making healthy farm-to-table food taste terrific. Her recipes were delicious, healthy, and surprisingly easy to follow. We hired her on the spot. It was the best business decision in my adult life. And I just learned another one of the most important lessons that it takes to become a successful entrepreneur. Hire people who are not just better than yourself but much better at their chosen domain. Silicon Valley celebrates full-stack engineers that can do anything. However, what I'd missed up to this point was having a truly extraordinary Head of Product, in this case food, who instinctively knew what consumers wanted. Instead of taking years to get product market fit, we got it right off the bat. Chef Justine was that good. She was my Jonathan Ive.

While there were a million things left to do to get the healthy food start-up off the ground, there were two important things to take care of first. One, I went confidently to my lead investor, Tim, and walked him through the new business model and why it was so much better than Lasso's. I went to my banker, Albert, at Silicon Valley Bank and did the same. I was terrified that they'd both tell me no. That I wasn't allowed to pivot the business. That pivoting the business meant failure. They did ask me hard questions, but because I'd built my $100 million business model with solid assumptions, I was able to answer their questions easily. They were impressed, said they loved the new idea, thought it was much better than Lasso, and encouraged me to immediately focus all my energy on it. They wouldn't give me new money until it was up and rolling, but if I wanted to go lean for a bit, i.e., not take a salary and reduce my company's burn, they were happy to be supportive (in Silicon Valley Bank's case, not call the loan) and go on this new adventure with me. I said, of course, and we were off to the races.

The other thing we needed was a name. Tyler and I had by this point started running the hills of Marin together. Our favorite run we called a "sun run" because we tried to run to the top of a trail called Miwok before the sun came out. Tyler was taller, younger, and a much better runner that I was. However, I was supercompetitive and determined not to let him beat me. I'd surreptitiously run the trail multiple times during the week by myself so that when Tyler and I ran it together on the weekend I could actually beat him. It was good-natured rivalry, and it was a great time to get to know each other.

To hear his stories about growing up on a farm. About winning *The Amazing Race*. About his struggle to find himself after the race, since he'd been a success so early in life. About his dream of having a family. About my fear of having one. I told him how much I loved Christina and how afraid I was to have a child. He told me I had to have a child. No ifs, ands, or buts. I'd be a great father. I'd love it. It would be the most amazing thing in my life. I couldn't let Christina go.

Having hung out with guys for years that were totally focused on partying. On booze. On hitting on girls. It felt great to be with someone so positive. So healthy. So full of life. So family centered. I decided to agree with Tyler in my mind, and things started to change. I felt more positive inside. I felt more confident inside. I felt like these sun runs were my weekly therapy. What was transforming me from the inside out. And then it hit me.

Tyler was like a Sun God. Like the Greek god Hermes who could run at supersonic speeds. Our sun runs were this magical thing. When we got to the top of the mountain right as the sun poked over the clouds and its brilliant rays spread across the sky, I could think of nothing more magical. More amazing. I wanted my company to feel just like the feeling I was having at that moment with Tyler. And I said to Tyler, the word "sun" has to part of our company name. Tyler said Sun Box, and I raced home to tell Christina the name and she hated it. For obvious reasons the word "box" didn't resonate with her, and she didn't think it would resonate with other females either. It sounded crudely sexual to her. Not healthy at all. I moped around the apartment for a few hours when the name came to me. A better word than box to affix to the word Sun. We'd name our company Sun Basket. I immediately got online, and my heart raced with anticipation as I searched to see if the URL sunbasket.com was available to buy. Surprisingly it was for about one thousand dollars. For people not in the online industry, getting a real business name you can spell and say and that feels good is like spotting a unicorn in your backyard. I called Tyler and announced with giddy anticipation that I'd just bought the name Sun Basket. Luckily, he loved the name just as much as I did. And I learned yet another lesson that's often missed when young new entrepreneurs start online companies. Your name matters. It's going to be the one word that every new customer first hears when they learn about your company. It's going to be the first word new prospective employees hear when they hear about a new job opportunity. It needs to be relatable. Easy to spell. Broad enough to encompass your long-term vision but narrow enough to resonate with what your product is today. I'd just stumbled upon the perfect name for our new healthy food company. I'll write it again as I like it that much. Sun Basket. It stood for all good things under the sun. Our mantra was that eating healthy food helped you nourish your body from the inside out. It helped you be your best self. It helped you shine.

CHAPTER 9

Planet: Healing the Earth: The World Wide Web Starts with You

We started Sun Basket in Tyler's kitchen, because my previous product concept, Lasso, had drained the company's bank account and we didn't have enough money to rent a proper office. It was actually a lot more fun that way. And zanier. Tyler had one simple rule as he gave me a key to his apartment. I needed to always call ahead of time before I let myself in. So that I wouldn't walk in on him or one of his roommates, including his soon-to-be wife, naked. Since that's the way they rolled. He said it in a straightforward way. Not joking. And I totally believed him after years of watching Tyler follow his own path in life. Having watched his zany ways.

It was a huge kitchen with a big butcher block for a counter. The chef would create recipes at the stove while George and Tyler worked on how to make the first box that we could ship our Sun Basket food in. None of us had any idea how to create such a box, and the first one was, like many first tries that a new start-up creates, both super funny and terrible.

I was sitting at home one day when a box arrived that had written in magic marker on it, "Sun Basket—Wildly Delicious Food Inside" written in magic marker with a huge exclamation point next to it. I smiled, looking at the hand-drawn letters and cringed a bit since I was an over-forty-year-old serial entrepreneur realizing how far we still had to go. Nevertheless, I opened the box and inside, all the food items had been jumbled from transit. Wanting to make the first box extra special, Tyler and George had included a Tecate beer, which I wisely opened over the sink, because it sprayed all over the place.

The instructions were neatly typed, and the food was carefully wrapped. I went to the stove, laid out the ingredients, and cooked as the company's first customer, Sun Basket #1. If I remember correctly, it was a stuffed eggplant dish, and it was absolutely terrific. Despite the bad packaging, the jumbled mess of ingredients inside, and the temperature control problems of the box, Chef Justine's amazing talent for creating simple, delicious, healthy recipes shone through. My nervousness about the box and all the other things fell away. Because by this time, I'd learned another super-important Silicon Valley lesson. While the business model was important, the number one thing that made a company successful was the product. Let me say that again. It's all about the product. Nothing else is more important once your business model is solid. Not the packaging. Not your website. Not your operations. Not your marketing. While if any one of those things, if not amazing or well executed, can ruin a business, without a great product there is no path to greatness, period.

I'm sure you're thinking about companies where they somehow made a profit without a great product. And I'm sure you'll be able to come up with a few examples. But I challenge you to come up with a truly great company that didn't have a truly great product that lasted the test of time. All my favorite companies and CEO heroes have gotten one thing fundamentally right. They make awesome products. Apple—world's best computers and iPhones. Google—world's best search platform. Amazon—world's best e-commerce marketplace. Patagonia—world's best outdoor sporting gear. Tesla—world's best car, not just electric car, period. It was always the same. With Chef Justine, I'd finally found my Jonathan Ive who, as long as I nurtured our relationship carefully, I had 100 percent confidence that together, we—and what would turn into a team over time of seventeen hundred people—could create an amazing company. One that did good by doing good.

And it was that second part that really struck a nerve with the press. With new employees. With our customers. An idea popped into my head as we were starting Sun Basket that, yes, our goal was to make good food. But what we were really doing was making food good. Good for our bodies. Good for our souls. Good for our planet. That one position shift of the word "good," from making good food to making food good, changed everything. It gave us a mission. It gave us a reason for being. It gave me the platform to stand in front of journalists and bloggers and investors and say that Sun Basket's mission was to help change the world. By making food a force for good. And the press and bloggers and investors loved it. They secretly all felt the same way. They were embarrassed by all the junk food they put in their bodies. They felt guilty about the bad food they sometimes fed their families when they were in a hurry. They, like me, often felt out of control when they got too busy and stopped exercising. Stopped eating healthy. Grabbed whatever was in the freezer. The burrito. The frozen pizza. Anything but what was natural and healthy.

We had an amazing experience when we were getting started where we hired a comedy troupe to help us gain insights into what customers wanted for dinner. I know what you must be thinking: *What does a comedy troupe have to do with food?* It seems like I'm about to tell you a bad joke with a cheesy punch line. But the comedy group was led by a former advertising savant named Paul, who had a wicked sense of humor and was also a kind, great human being and was good friends with my co-founder George.

George, who towers above all of us at over 6'5" was a really funny, gentle giant. He'd grown up in Marin, lived the healthy real food lifestyle, and was and is super creative. In his twenties and thirties, like me and Tyler, he'd focused on making movies. Then he'd joined me for multiple of my company adventures, including Zannel, del.icio.us, and Lasso. He'd always held back a bit of his zany creative ideas, and he was convinced this time that we needed to do things a bit differently. Not just come up with a product idea and make it. But instead try to plum insights from customers. From real people. And since we both didn't want to do focus groups, which sounded very businesslike and boring, although they can have great value when used correctly, he convinced me to hire his friend Paul's comedy group to help us.

We arrived at the nondescript workspace in the heart of the Mission neighborhood. The comedians were already getting worked up about food puns. They were making puns back and forth at each other. They were excited to pair together to avoid coming up with something cheesy that would grate on our users' nerves. I cringed a bit, since puns were the furthest thing from what I thought would resonate with our users. But before I could say anything, both George and Paul assured me that it was going to be a great session. Paul's comedians were just warming up their mental muscles the same way that a musician plays scales before she plays a recital.

We all sat down, and Paul stood in front of us. He told us the ground rules. There were no bad ideas. If there were bad ideas, then they were to be cherished. We were entering a safe space. Tonight, we were going to find out together why we ate dinner. What it meant to us. How Sun Basket could help. It was going to be funny. Fun. An irreverent time. Unlike any other product development workshop we'd ever experienced, and it was.

He started by asking his comedians to yell out words that came to mind when they thought about dinner. All sorts of words came surging out. Guilt. Same old stir-ry. Fridge to mouth. And so on. I was listening with rapt fascination while these creative people that I'd never met before yelled out one little precious insight after another. Next, we role-played some of the best ideas. The fridge-to-mouth one was really fun. It was a short improve skit where the comedians plus a few of my team members showed what it was like when they came home from work and they were super hungry. Tired. Wanted something to eat but were too lazy to cook a complex meal. They went straight to the fridge. They peered inside. I still remember the two actors dramatically opening the imaginary fridge door and then staring inside. They looked like human varmints ravenous for their next meal. Then, all of a sudden, one of them pulled out of the imaginary fridge an imaginary jar of peanut butter. One of them unscrewed the top while the other one rummaged for more delicious unhealthy stuff in the fridge to eat. And then they did it. They both started to eat fridge-to-mouth. It was super funny. It was a bit over the top. But they had just illustrated a keen insight that we would have totally missed if we had gone about things the traditional way. People when they were hungry went straight to their fridge. They forgot all their good eating behaviors. They forgot their restraint. They put their diet plans on hold. They let elemental hunger take over. We all laughed uproariously and clapped when the skit was over. It was dead-on since many of us had done our version of this ritual many times. Without even realizing it if we were lost in thought, thinking about work.

The amazing thing that came out of the night with the comedy group was how much they all wanted to eat healthy. How few of them felt that they had the tools to eat healthy for dinner. That dinner felt like a chore. That when they reverted to bad behaviors, like had happened in the fridge-to-mouth skit, that they went off the deep end. Straight to eating peanut butter from the jar. Straight to the freezer to take out frozen pizzas and burritos and heating them up in the microwave. There wasn't a middle ground between when they ate healthy, which for many of them meant the same old boring stir-fry, and when they ate super-indulgent food that tasted good but made them feel guilty since it was so unhealthy. This was the key insight. The same I'd experienced when I'd lost 50 pounds. If we could make healthy cooking easy and delicious. We had a hit. Two of the three brand pillars would make a good service, only all three would make a great one.

So, we were headed in the right direction but didn't want to sound preachy. Tyler and I debated over and over what slogans to put on our box. We wanted it to celebrate our commitment to the planet. To treating animals right. To treating your body right. To celebrating healthy food. However, we were struggling with how to reconcile our desire to brand ourselves as a healthy eating company and our aspiration to celebrate the farms from which our food came. And that's when we hit a second key insight. Again, by talking to real customers about what they cared about.

We were sitting around a small table having an informal focus group, what I like to call a "pizza and beer" focus group. Not because you served pizza and beer, especially at my healthy food company, but because it was informal. Not overly processed. There were no professional moderators there. I asked one of the participants how he picked the eggs he purchased at the grocery store, and he told me a story that became part of the core DNA of Sun Basket.

He said that when he went to the egg aisle, he looked at each of the egg containers and tried to imagine the farm where the chickens were raised. If he could imagine a bucolic farm where the chickens were treated humanely. Where the farmer did things right. And if he also was able to read that the eggs had all the no's, then that was the egg carton he'd buy. I asked what the "no's" meant, and he immediately responded: no antibiotics, no hormones, no preservatives, no anything except that they were just real eggs. Real food.

And then it struck me. As a team, we were creating a false divide between what we were calling healthy food and farm-to-table food. They were the same thing. While the fitness industry had taken over the word healthy, and many people had negative associations to it—such as health supplements, health vitamins, and health food that looked like gruel—what our customers associated with healthy food was food that was directly from farms. That had nothing bad in it. That was preservative free. Hormone free. Antibiotic free. What they wanted, before the phrase became all the recent rage, was clean food.

The images to put on the side of the box and the phrases with it came immediately. We created a panel with a playful-looking cow and wrote, "Responsibly Raised, Room to Moo." We created another panel of a fisherperson and added the phrase, "Wild Caught, Wildly Delicious." For clarity, after much discussion about it sounding too "on the nose," we added anyway "From the Best Farms to Your Table." On our website, we were the first food delivery company to add a Values section as a top navigation item. We wanted customers to know what we stood for. That health food was of course about the nutrients that we put into our family's bodies. But it was also more than that. It was how we treated our community. How we treated the team of people that worked for us. How we treated the animals that fed us. How we needed to be good stewards of the land.

And I'd learned another huge life and business lesson. That in the new economy, the best way to grow your business was by doing well by doing good. By caring for our shared planet. For realizing that the World Wide Web is of course an Internet phenomenon. But more importantly, it is a human phenomenon. It is what unites us. What brings us together. That we are all in this thing called life together. That we must treat each other with respect. When we treat our neighbors with respect. When we treat the planet with kindness, then we pay forward all the wonderful things that have been given to us. Not that the world is perfect. Far from that. We live in a time of unprecedented political corruption. Multiple wars fought in foreign lands. Terrorism. Famine. A good portion of the world, despite the riches of the world economy, going hungry. But rather than just repeat these terrible truths over and over to ourselves, that it was up to us to be part of the solution. Not the problem. To stand up for ourselves. Stand up for our planet. To each do it in our own way.

I was far from perfect. In my life I'd done as many things wrong as I'd done right. However, for the first time with Sun Basket, I knew that I was on the path to creating something really good. Something where, if I did it right, I could in my own way have a positive impact on the planet. I knew that I wasn't solving all the world's food problems, particularly since Sun Basket was expensive and, at least at the beginning, would service the people who least needed it. However, I was no longer sitting on the sidelines. I had a big vision of how I wanted to improve people's everyday lives by helping them learn to cook and eat healthy, delicious, easy meals. We'd join the battle to fight America's fast food and obesity epidemic one healthy meal at time.

CHAPTER 10

Sky: Soaring High into the Sky: From Failsafe Entrepreneur to Freedom

"Adam, you're what I call a failsafe entrepreneur."

I sat across from a Frenchman who was a journalist turned VC turned back to a writer. We were sitting on the roof of the building where my start-up, Sun Basket, was growing rapidly. The sun was blazing down, and it was a glorious day. I looked out at the San Francisco skyline and marveled at how fortunate I felt that Sun Basket was going well. In a city where the pressure was intense. To perform. To grow. To succeed. Or you would wither away, and another start-up would come to take your place on its pilgrimage to ascend the huge heights that a technology company, when it worked, could achieve.

I didn't like the word "failsafe" even though I wasn't sure what it meant yet. It had the word "fail" in it that I thought couldn't be good. Perhaps I shouldn't have taken this interview from a VC who had previously turned me down. I'd met him about a year before when I was still doing Lasso, after he tried to recruit me to be CEO of one of his start-ups. I'd told him I was doing Lasso, and he'd heard my pitch. And then like twenty other VCs before him, he'd thanked me for sharing my idea with him but had told me in a kind way that it was not a fit for his firm.

Here we were a year later, and boy had things changed for me, I thought. I'd shut down Lasso after the first month that we launched Sun Basket. Because in that first month of Sun Basket's existence it had grown like a rocket ship. It had grown more in less than thirty days than Lasso had grown in two years. And everyone who tried Sun Basket loved it.

The first really trying moment when we were unveiling Sun Basket came when a journalist for the *San Francisco Chronicle* who knew Chef Justine asked if she could profile Sun Basket. She wanted to include it in a piece she was doing on meal kits. While this newfangled idea had really caught on along the East Coast, since that's where Blue Apron and other competitors started, it was still a relatively new phenomenon here. What intrigued the journalist was that we were the first meal kit to add a pedigree chef as our Head of Product and the first one that was totally focused on health.

I was thrilled that the journalist wanted to cover us. There was just one problem. We weren't ready. We didn't have the illustration done for our box. We'd just gotten the first draft of our website done. It had potential but still had lots of bugs to fix. And the recipes still took too long. I got on the phone with the journalist and listened as she told me about the article she wanted to write. It sounded great. I really wanted Sun Basket to be in it, since it was going to be on the front page of the food section of one of the Bay Area's most important newspapers. However, I was also terrified because of everything that could go wrong. With the box. With the website breaking. With all the things we hadn't polished yet.

I decided, like I have many times in my life when confronted with ambiguity, to be brutally honest with the journalist. I told her that I really wanted to be in her story. I told her what made us different. I spoke to her passionately about how I'd lost 50 pounds by changing my diet and now wanted to help others find their path to living a much healthier life with food as their medicine. The challenge, I told her when she asked if she could try our product, was that we simply weren't ready yet. The box she'd receive would just have a sticker on the side of it, not the cool illustration that we were working on. The website wasn't working right yet. It was janky. The recipe photos, while they looked good, were currently being done by interns. We hadn't hired a professional photographer yet. All that said, I told her, as I took a deep breath, the one thing that I knew for sure was that the recipes—our core product—were absolutely amazing. So, if she could overlook everything else, I was confident that she'd have an amazing cooking experience. The journalist kindly said that of course all she cared about was the product. The cooking experience. I agreed to send her a box, got her address, and we hung up.

I got off the phone and everyone who was in the room, particularly one of the women on my marketing team with a background in PR, said that I'd just been had by a savvy journalist. She'd told me what I wanted to hear. I'd been too honest. Oh boy! This could be it. We could get roasted by a major newspaper before we even shipped our first product to real customers.

I had an uneasy feeling that they might be right. That I'd been played. But I had really liked the journalist. I believed that life was better lived trusting people. Not naively, but when your gut said that they were good people. More importantly, I had been cooking Chef Justine's meals, and I knew that they were that good. Better than anything I'd ever made myself at home. Better than almost all the restaurants I went to. Save a few that had a similar farm-to-table approach and celebrated the freshest foods with healthy, delicious sauces.

Because delicious sauce was the thing that made Sun Basket different when we first started. Our simple marketing statement was that "we made healthy cooking easy and delicious." What we'd found was that was a hard thing to do. Until Chef Justine had come to the team and said what if we ship them ingredients plus a delicious sauce. Instead of forcing our customers to make the sauce, the most complicated part, we'd make it for them. Help them turn an ordinary meal into an extraordinary one by adding a delicious sauce. A romesco sauce. A harissa sauce. All those amazing sauces that you took for granted when you went to an amazingly good, healthy restaurant but would never have the time or skill to make for yourself at home.

And then the newspaper hit the stands. At 6:00 A.M. that morning I went out to buy a newspaper from one of the local news vendors. I had never done that. I normally just read my news obsessively online. But I wanted the feel of the newsprint on my fingers. I wanted to read the article the old-fashioned way, even though I knew that I could much more easily just go to the *Chronicle* website and read it online.

I brought the newspaper back to my apartment and laid it out on my big wooden dining room table. I took my time unfolding the sections of the newspaper until I found the food section. It had taken me a couple of tries to find the section of the newspaper, since I hadn't read a physical newspaper since I was a kid.

And there it was. There was a huge photo of a delicious looking meal on the front page of the food section. My eyes looked at the dense newsprint as they raced down the page. Reading about a couple of the other meal services first. Searching to find the section where she reviewed Sun Basket. So far, the journalist had been pretty good to the other kit services, I thought. That seemed like a good omen, I thought. And then I found it. The part of the article about us. My heart raced even faster. I was nervous. For a moment, I thought to myself that it had been the worst idea in the world to let this journalist try our food when we clearly weren't ready. We had nowhere near the same level of polish as all the other services she'd just reviewed and I'd read about. I had a sinking feeling in my gut. I wanted to close the newspaper and not read it. To go back into my entrepreneurial cave and keep working with the team on the product versus exposing what we'd just created to the world. I had entrepreneur stage fright. Which was never good. But in this case, I felt it was justified. Because we weren't ready. Because I'd taken a risk trusting this journalist. Who sounded nice, but in truth I didn't know her.

I couldn't avoid it anymore, so I started to read. I was pleasantly surprised that she'd gotten our positioning around health right. I also liked that she spoke in semi-reverential terms about Chef Justine, who was a chef's chef in the world of the San Francisco food industry. She wasn't a household name, at least not yet, like Tyler Florence or other

Food Network celebrity chefs, but she was the real deal. A self-trained, incredible chef. The best product person I've ever worked with, period. And here was my moment of truth. I realized I should be feeling confident inside. I had the real goods. If this journalist was being true to our conversation, there was no way she could write something bad about our meal experience because Chef Justine was that good. I began to feel hope when I read the last section of the article that described her experience cooking her Sun Basket meal.

And there it was, the journalist used the word "skeptical." My heart sank again. The journalist related that she'd decided for Sun Basket that she would put it to the hardest test of all the meal kits. She'd cook a meal with one of her friends who hated the concept of meal kits. Who thought meal kits were antithetical to the slow food movement. That it went against all the tenets her friend stood for. Shopping for real food among real people at a farmers' market. Not ordering something online. Carefully selecting a recipe from your favorite, dog-eared cookbook. Not getting the recipe sent to you like riding a bike with training wheels. I prepared myself for the worst. I set down the newspaper for a moment and paced around the room. I knew it. *I knew it*, I told myself. I should have listened to the woman on my marketing team who came from the world of PR. I'd let myself become gullible. I'd handed over my prized new possession. My new start-up's product when it wasn't ready. I'd violated every tenet of what I'm sure Steve Jobs would say if he'd given me advice about how to start my company. Never, oh never, show your product until it's absolutely ready. Don't fall into the trap of trying to get publicity before it's ready.

I went back and picked up the newspaper despondently. Ughhh. I couldn't believe how foolish I'd been. All in the euphoric moment of feeling great about my new product. I was positive I'd made possibly a game-ending mistake. And then I read the final paragraph.

The journalist said that despite her friend's initial skepticism about meal kits, they'd had an incredible time cooking the Sun Basket meal together. More importantly, her friend said that the Sun Basket meal was possibly the most delicious meal she'd had in a long while.

Holy cow! I started to dance around my room. Wow! We'd gotten the best coverage of any of the other meal kit offerings by far. I felt vindicated. I felt awesome because I knew I had been right to pick Chef Justine. My despondency turned to elation as I knew that thousands of readers of the *Chronicle* would come and start pounding on our website door to let them in. Let them try Sun Basket, and that's just what they did.

"What does failsafe entrepreneur mean?" I asked the French journalist who was sitting across from me. I was annoyed that he had used the word "fail" to describe me. It seemed presumptuous, because he didn't even know me that well. Sure, we'd had a great couple of conversations when I'd visited his VC firm. Sure, I really liked that, like me, he had a creative background before he'd gone into the world of business. But boy did it bother me that he was using the word "fail" in part to describe me.

While it was fine if to myself I felt like I was a failure, it was something entirely different to have someone else say that about me. And right now, to be honest, I wasn't feeling like a failure. For the first time in a long while, I was feeling good about my career. Confident. Like I was on the right track.

The last year had been a whirlwind of success. We'd gotten product market fit with service immediately. Something that I'd never gotten before in my life and which I ascribed to the fact that I'd partnered with an incredibly experienced product person versus trying to do it myself, something that I'd done in previous start-ups that had capped their potential. We'd also hit a nerve with our focus on healthy, clean eating. Consumers loved the idea. Craved having a service that made dinners healthy, easy, and delicious.

As obvious as that sounds, when we first started, my Head of Marketing at the time told me that I couldn't position Sun Basket around health. She'd worked at some of the largest food companies in the United States, and they'd all come to the same conclusion: The word "health" or other words that implied health didn't sell. She brought up the example of the McLean Burger that McDonald's had launched. McDonald's had tried to do the right thing by creating a burger that was healthier for you. However, their consumers had rejected it. When the fast food company had changed the name of the McLean Burger to something that sounded delicious, its sales had spiked. Without changing the recipe. Just positioning the burger around being juicy. Delicious. Irresistibly tasty. Anything but healthy.

However, that had been years ago. And things had changed. I knew this both in my heart, and I also knew it because I'd been carefully studying the data. I had the funny quotes from the comedy group focus group. I had the story from the person who told me how he bought eggs at the store. As importantly, I had real data from customers online that we'd been testing different join flow messages with. Which all showed the same thing. Words like "healthy," "organic," "non-GMO," "clean," "paleo," "gluten-free" were hits. People made it through to the last step of the join flow, which was to purchase our product, five times more often than if we just focused on how tasty the food was. Not that the word "delicious" wasn't important. We knew that without the food being delicious we wouldn't last a month as an online food company. However, it wasn't the main reason people were coming. They were showing up at our site in droves, even before we released it officially in public, because we promised very clearly one thing. A healthy, delicious meal.

The French journalist turned VC turned writer adjusted himself on the rooftop couch and smiled at me. He'd guessed that I might not like the word "fail" as part of the way he believed was appropriate to describe me. But before I jumped to any conclusions, he wanted to share with me what he meant. And he promised me it was a good thing.

He told me that over the past year he'd interviewed dozens of entrepreneurs. He'd studied even more of their careers from afar. What he'd learned had surprised him. While some of the truly transcendent entrepreneurs were overnight sensations, like Chad and Steve, when they had a runaway product. That wasn't the case for most successful entrepreneurs. Most of them, he'd found out, were what he called excellent craftsmen and craftswomen. They'd worked on their trade, entrepreneurship, over a long period of time before they'd become successful.

Like anything that was really hard to do at the highest level, whether it was being a professional athlete, a professional musician, or in this case a professional entrepreneur, most failed numerous times before they succeeded. What made me different was how I failed, he said. According to this French author, many entrepreneurs, when they failed, failed spectacularly. They not only lost all their venture capitalists' money, but they also burned bridges with their investors by getting into unnecessary fights in the boardroom at the end.

Their start-ups crashed and burned so hard when it didn't work that many of these entrepreneurs struggled to get their employees to work with them again. Because they weren't transparent with their board or their employees about what was working or not working. Because they were not test driven and honest with themselves. Because they didn't manage their finite VC funds well. Because frankly they took too much risk before they had product market fit. They didn't have any notion of safety.

In contrast, the French journalist turned VC turned writer told me that is what made me different. What made me part of an elite group of unsuccessful entrepreneurs was that I failed safely. I cringed when he said the phrase "elite group of unsuccessful entrepreneurs" since it sounded like an oxymoron to me. There was nothing elite about being unsuccessful. I began to resent the man who was sitting across from me. I felt he was using fanciful words to, intentionally or not, ridicule me. That it was pure sophistry that there was any benefit to me in being associated with a group of people that, in my mind, he was essentially calling losers.

I ended the meeting on pleasant terms and said that I looked forward to reading his book, even though I was seething inside. I wasn't a failsafe entrepreneur. I had been a risk taker my whole life. It was easy for him to think I was safe, sitting from his perch as a VC and writer. Someone who had been a critic all his life, I thought, versus someone in the trenches like me taking risk. It wasn't until much later, two years after we met on the roof and his book had just come out, that I realized the nuanced vision of the failsafe entrepreneur. He wasn't trying to criticize me. Or say that I wasn't entrepreneurial enough. Quite the opposite. What he was saying was that entrepreneurship, when it's sustained as a career versus a flash-in-the-pan success, takes real work. It takes approaching it like a craft. Just like you would approach becoming a doctor. A lawyer. A scientist. Sure, anyone could label themselves an entrepreneur since there were no board exams you had to take. But there was a huge chasm between those who practiced the art and craft of entrepreneurship successfully and those who never got out of the starting gate.

And this is where I learned another important life lesson. Something that I realized I had been doing the whole time, but never realized consciously that I was doing. That I had put a premium on learning. On listening to others as I built my start-ups versus believing that I knew all the answers. That I had put a premium on transparency. On letting my investors and my employees know what was working and not working. That I had put a premium on making sure, to the best of my ability, that if things didn't work out, that my investors and employees weren't left sweeping up the mess. When one of my ideas had spectacularly failed, I'd been the last person standing who had flipped off the power of our servers and given the keys to our building back to our landlord. No matter how much I'd wanted to, I hadn't run away. I'd faced failure head-on. Over and over. Until finally this relentless focus of trying to get better. Trying to do the right thing for my customers. For my employees. For my investors, set me free. Figuratively and literally.

It was two years later. Two years since the French author and I had last met. We sat across from each other again. His book had just come out and he wanted to know what I thought. He'd grown a beard. He had a cool, stark-looking image of himself in black and white on the back of the hardcover book. His book was well written. It was thoughtful. It included me in the final chapter, describing me as a failsafe entreprenuer. I no longer felt resentful. I felt good inside. That in all the years when things didn't work out, I had treated people the right way. I'd helped make sure that, when the idea failed, that we had done what in Silicon Valley is called a "soft landing." I'd made sure my employees got jobs. I'd made sure the VCs didn't have to pay any extra dollars to shut down the service except what they had already invested. It was this discipline that had given me the chance to practice my craft of entrepreneurship over and over until finally, with Sun Basket, I'd gotten it right.

All the things that needed to fall into place had happened. Great idea. Great timing. Great team. Great product. Great first article that had launched our company into a low orbit that just got higher and higher.

Over the course of the first two years of our business, we grew faster than Airbnb, Zappos, and Uber. We were written up in *Forbes, Fast Company, Entrepreneur, Inc, TechCrunch, The Wall Street Journal,* and a host of other publications. I got the opportunity, while we were still a private company, to ring the Nasdaq closing bell during their fitness week, the first week of January. It was one of the coolest experiences of my life as my team cheered. As my team counted down and then the digital bell rang. We ran outside. We saw ourselves on Nasdaq's jumbotron. We were all giddy with excitement about what we were creating. We'd gone from zero to $300 million in annual revenue run rate (ARR) and zero to 1,700 employees in less than four years. Customers loved us. Influencers v-blogged positively about us. My team felt inspired. Even my dad, who always had been overly critical of me, told me how impressed he was about what I'd done.

There would be incredibly hard challenges to come. We weren't done yet by any stretch of the imagination. However, for the first time in my life I felt totally free. Free from all the stress of starting a start-up. Free from the stress of failing. Free from the stress of having to explain to your investors and employees and friends that you were failing.

I told the French author that I was humbled that he included me in his book. I was a proud former "failsafe" entrepreneur. He asked what I meant, and I told him. I agreed with his book that there was a huge element of craftmanship in learning to become a successful entrepreneur. However, there was another step that I thought that his book was missing. It was about the freedom to jump off the tallest cliff you could find in business. In life. In whatever you choose to do. And to do it fearlessly. To know that there would be failure. But also, to know that through failure you could reach amazing new heights you never thought were possible. That beyond craftsmanship there was art. There was intuition. There were dreams that were a thousand times. A million times. A zillion times (I didn't say zillion, but I thought it to myself) bigger than mere craftsmanship. Knowing your craft was the table stakes to being good at any profession. However, when I had been studying writing years before, the one thing that had stuck with me the most is what a famous author had said, that first you have to learn the rules. Next you have to swallow them and then never think about them again. They were inside you. Fused together with your intuition. Until your skills and intuition became one. And you were guided again by the voice within you that now was even smarter and knew the direction that you should go. It was only at this point, when art and science connected completely within my brain, that I finally felt free. Whether or not I ultimately transcended to the highest halls of entrepreneurship and the business hall of fame, I'd already made it in my own mind. I no longer felt like a failure. For the first time I felt truly like a success. I felt like I'd come into my own. I was finally me.

CHAPTER 11

Eternity: Making the Universal Connection: Your Path to Eternal Sunshine

The French author thanked me for my time and thoughtful comments about his book, and he headed home. I sat by myself on the rooftop of the building where we'd just met. I felt the sun shining on my face. It's warmth. It's intensity. Feeling like the sun's energy was flowing from the top of my head down into my body. Down through my veins. Across my arms. Down my legs. Until it tickled my toes. I felt good inside. I felt whole.

I had created a company called Sun Basket, in large part inspired by Tyler and my Sun Runs. I had named the company Sun Basket inspired in large part also by my friend Tyler, also who, like I said before, looked like a sun god. And now, years later, Sun Basket was a success. We were shipping over a million Sun Basket meals to customers per month. We were shipping, in my mind, boxes that had the goodness of the earth trapped inside. We were exporting the best of Northern California, where I lived and worked, to the rest of the country. We were shipping our customers, I imagined boxes full of sun. Boxes that, when you opened them, were full of the sun's energy. Full of food grown directly under the sun. Food that, when you put it into your body, turned into energy. Made the molecules, the cells, the things that make your bodily functions go.

It was then that it hit me. The most important lesson of all. That we're all connected. Every one of us. To each other. To the planet. To the animals around us. To the streams. To the mountains. To the birds. To the rushing of the wind around us. Why? Because at the elemental level, we're all made of the same thing. Protein, carbohydrates, and fat. At the elemental level, we all need the same thing to go. We all need energy. In our purest form we are energy. And where do we get that? From the sun.

It was a mind-blowing thought as I sat thinking about this on the rooftop, and it was a thought that I'd later learn my friends learned when they participated in an ayahuasca ceremony. For those not familiar with ayahuasca, it is a drug that is made from all-natural ingredients and has been used since ancient times to let people connect with their higher selves. To connect with the world around them. Full disclosure: I've never taken the drug or attended an ayahuasca ceremony. The experience that my friends related felt so similar to how I felt in that moment as I was sitting on the rooftop after talking to the French journalist that I had to mention it. I had to describe what this kindred group of souls felt when they partook in an ayahuasca ceremony.

If you have heard about ayahuasca, you probably know that when you take the drug, it involves self-purging. You literally throw up. You may have diarrhea. That is what I would view as the unpleasant part of the experience. However, the liberating part of the experience is that it is through this self-purging that you eliminate the toxins in your body. The things that are holding you back in life. The negative thoughts. The scar tissue from former relationships. The fear of following your dream. Whatever it is that keeps you from moving forward in your life. Keeps you from connecting to the ones that you love. To telling them that you love them. Care about them. And realizing that we're all in this together.

Let me say that again. We're all in this together. I know that's hard to realize when you turn on the news and every day you read in the newspaper or watch on television a politician say something that goes against every fiber of your being. When you see things on TV that are terrible. The senseless wars in the Middle East. That go on and on. The fights over oil. Over conflicting religious beliefs. Over land. The parts of the world that are still afflicted by famine. The huge percentage of the population in the United States, an overall very rich first world country, that goes to bed hungry each night. The amount of divisiveness in Washington, DC. The separation that it feels like gets greater and greater each day between the Left and the Right. The haves and the have-nots. Between a society that feels like it is splintering apart due to the marginalization of those who are less fortunate.

And that's the problem. That's the thing we as a civilization must strive to overcome. To never let all the things that separate us, divide us. No, we all need to individually decide, one person at a time, that that which divides us also unites us. It's not some new age gobbledygook that one of the things that makes life worth living is learning about people who different from you. Who have different beliefs. Different life experiences. Different ways of raising their family. Cooking food. Living their life. Think about it. That's why we travel. That's why we study abroad, if we're fortunate enough to do so when we're in college. That's why the founding fathers, when they created the Declaration of Independence and the Constitution, stipulated to the best of their ability that we were all equal under the eyes of God. And like I've previously said, I don't mean a God that has a long gray beard and looks like Charlton Heston. No, what I mean is an intelligent life force. The laws of nature. The laws of physics. That for every reaction there is an equal reaction. The yin and yang of life. That life, as my good friend said, is more interesting if there is a God. If there is a larger purpose to our collective lives than just that we live and we die.

Of course, we have five senses. We experience each one of them every day. And it's important to stay grounded and learn all about the world using these five senses. To feel the warmth of the sun on your skin. To behold the amazing sights of nature in its most glorious forms. Hiking to the top of impossibly high waterfalls. Racing down the narrows of a red rock valley on a mountain bike. To smell the first flowers bloom when spring comes. To taste an exquisitely crafted meal, with the subtle complexity of the flavors, when you visit France. Or Italy. Or Indonesia. Or New Guinea. That you fall in love with another person. That you feel the touch of their skin as you lay curled up together under the blankets on a cold winter's night. That you go to the symphony and listen to incredibly gifted musicians play some of the most amazing music that's ever been written.

To do each and every one of those things is to be human. To live a full life. If you are so lucky. If you, like me, grow up fortunate to have the means to do them. To travel. To dine at great restaurants. To watch amazing performances. To spend time hiking in the forest. And so on.

But that is not enough. Not nearly enough. To truly be human, as I've said before, is to not only consume what the earth and others have made but to create as well. To put something out into the world that creates energy. Not just consumes energy. This was one of the fundamental insights that hit me as I was sitting up on the roof thinking about Sun Basket. That, sure, there were tons of things in my life that I still needed to work on. Still needed to improve. But for the first time in my life, I felt like I was on the right side of history. The right side of living the good life. In my own small way. I was creating boxes filled with sunlight. Boxes filled with energy. For every negative action on the planet, there could be a positive one. That I could be part of that positivity. I could be part of those rays of sunlight.

Because that is what the sun stands for for me. It stands for positivity. It stands for another new day. A new beginning after a long, long night. And there is nothing wrong with darkness. The absence of light. Without it, we would not know sunlight. As one of my mother's psychologist friends once told me, hate is what makes us understand love. It's hard to love someone if you've never experienced hate. Even for a split second. Since it is that feeling of negatively that lets you understand its opposite. To feel the love that you are capable of. Toward yourself. Toward your family. Toward your daughter or son. Toward your mother and father. Toward your friends. Toward strangers. Toward humanity.

And before you stop reading and say that all sounds like a bunch of nonsense, ask yourself a simple question. When do you feel most happy inside? When you are fighting with your sister? When you are filled with hate toward a political group whose beliefs are the opposite of your own? When you almost get hit by another driver and you are filled with rage? Filled at that moment with wanting to bash the other car in. Or is it when you are alone in the forest? Walking among the coolness of the trees. When you feel the cool breeze on your face. When you feel connected to something greater around you. When you feel things have a reason for being. That there is a natural order to things. If you listen to that voice deep down in you that guides you. That if you listen to it helps connect you to the worldwide web around you.

As I near the end of my book, I hope hearing my story has in some small way been helpful to you. And to that end, there is just one more story. One more experience that irrevocably changed my life that I want to share with you. That helped me realize that we're all in this together. That there's something larger. More important than just yourself. That when you listen at the deepest level to your Inner Voice, it connects you at the most fundamental level to everything that's all around you.

When I was twenty years old, I studied abroad in Germany. Why Germany? Because when I'd been in high school, the German class was in the afternoon and Spanish had been in the morning. I preferred getting up a bit later, and it turned out that my overly logical brained liked the sentence structure of the Germanic language. Flash forward to now I'm twenty years old and I've recently arrived in Germany. I don't know anyone, so I naively think to myself what would be a great way to meet all the other Germans in my dorm since I don't want to sit in my room all day by myself. I decide to go buy some beer at the local store nearby and start handing out free beer in the dorm kitchen. Not surprisingly, in a few hours, I'm friends with pretty much everyone in the dorm. Not because of any great insight on my part. Not because Germans like to drink beer any more than Americans do. But because I took a moment to make a simple human connection. More importantly, I began to meet a group of people who'd grown up in a world very different from my own.

I became good friends with one of the Germans in particular. His name was Joerg. He liked to call himself the diminutive of his name, which he told me was Joergili. He and I became fast friends. Unlike me, he and his friends had grown up in a post–World War environment where the Germans, he explained to me, felt a huge sense of collective guilt. That the wrong that had been committed against the Jews and others that German troops had killed was part of their collective guilt. Part of their collective shame. It was up to Joerg and his generation to right the wrong. To make up for that terrible act. Looking back on it, how he felt then is exactly how I feel now. That every action in the universe has an equal reaction. That the act of war. The acts of butchery. The acts of mass genocide that had been done by his forefathers were beyond awful. However, Joerg's generation, no matter how much they wanted to, could not change what had come before. But they could have the opposite reaction. They could stand for goodness. They could create lives that were worth living. They could help those that were less fortunate. Have you ever wondered when you watch Angela Merkel on TV, why she seems so much more enlightened than many of our US politicians? While I don't know her personally, and I'm sure if I was a political scientist I'd find many flaws in her policies, what I was struck by was a humanness about how the young Germans of my generation approached the rest of the world at a collective level. Sure, there were people full of hate in Germany. People who were on the far right. But, in general, what I found when I visited Germany was that there was a collective group of people who welcomed immigrants to come to their country. Welcomed the less fortunate in. That agreed to re-unify with East Germany. Even though that cost them real money. Increased their taxes. Reduced their standard of living. Because it was the right thing to do. Because they shared a common history. A history that was full of rights and wrongs. Paths that shouldn't ever have been taken. Terrible acts of war that could never be forgiven. But also, amazing beautiful things. Works of art that were amazing. Castles like Neuschwanstein, a popular tourist destination, that felt like they were straight out of a book of fairy tales. While perhaps the person behind Neuschwanstein had been demented and half crazy, he'd created something that was wonderous in the world. That for every negative action, his craziness, something different, something good had emerged. While my father was Jewish and had been deeply skeptical of me studying abroad in Germany. I knew I was onto something. It felt right.

And it was when I was in Germany that I had a few of these miraculous experiences myself. When I counted on something larger than myself to guide my way. To save me from my self. After becoming friends with the Germans in my dorm, the group of Americans who were part of my program were taken by our instructors down to a small mountain town called Kleinwalsertal.

It was a ski village right on the border between Austria and Germany. And it looked and felt magical. As though I'd stepped back in time a few hundred years to a simpler time. When there weren't huge freeways. Enormous cars guzzling gas and barreling down ten-lane highways. No, this was a quaint town. A small one. Nestled up in the Austrian hills.

In the afternoon, we'd get together for German language lessons. In the evening we'd all go out for dinner and to drink delicious Austrian beer. During the mornings, we were left to explore and do what we wanted to do. And it was clear from the moment that I arrived what I was going to be doing from 8:00 A.M. to 2:00 P.M. every day. I was going to ski.

I'd grown up in Utah and started skiing when I was four years old. I fancied myself a good skier. Back home, I could ski black diamond. Double black diamond. Moguls. Powder. Tree ski, which meant between trees. I could handle crud, which meant bad snow. I'd worked hard my whole life to become what was called an "all mountain skier." Someone who could handle different terrains. Different slopes with different degrees of steepness.

And here I was for the first time out of the United States on my own. I was going to ski at one of Austria's famed ski resorts. And I was going to do it alone. Since I, as a smug twenty-year-old guy, reasoned that I was probably a better skier than everyone else. I didn't want to be held up by the other Americans who likely hadn't grown up skiing like I had in Utah. That hadn't grown up twenty minutes away from a ski hill. That hadn't grown up skiing at least twice a week. That hadn't had, as part of their classes, a day off during the week when, as a school group, we all went skiing together.

I bought my lift pass and then rode up the chair for the first ski lift that I saw. Then I rode up a second one. I marveled at how I was able to get on chair after chair that took me higher and higher up into the Austrian Alps. I had thousands of feet of vertical that I could ski down. Unlike the hills that I'd grown up skiing in Utah, these were even grander. Longer. Wow, was I going to have fun. I raced to the bottom and then decided that I wanted to do it again. Not take a break. Not go in for a hot drink. Not go in for lunch. No, I wanted to get back on the hill and do it all over again.

However, this time I was going to take the gondola that I'd seen on the way down. I was going to ride all the way to the top of the mountain. To a higher point than I'd been able to get to when I was just riding on the lift chairs. So, I went right over to the gondola, took off my skis, and climbed in. By myself. To take the gondola all the way to the top of the mountain. While of course there were other people in the other gondolas in front of and behind me, I blocked them out in my mind. It was just me and this huge beautiful mountain. For the next few hours, before I had to return for my afternoon German classes, it was just going to be me and this mountain.

I got off the gondola, knocked my poles together to clean off the snow on them, and stepped into my ski bindings. I heard both boots click in. I stretched my body left and then to the right. I bent over and felt my back stretch. And my back told me that it was ready to go down the hill, and then off I went.

For anyone who has never skied before, let me tell you it's one of the greatest feelings on earth. As you race down the hill making turn after turn, when things are going well and especially if there is powder on the hill, you feel like you are floating. Like you are skiing over the tops of clouds. Like you are weightless. Like you are soaring like a bird. I've done a lot of sports, from surfing to hiking to running to playing competitive sports in school, and I've never found anything that comes close to skiing. To the sense of freedom you feel when it is just you, a pair of skis, and the hill for a brief moment in time, all connected together.

And I was going fast. Faster than I normally skied in Utah. Why? Because no one was on the mountain that day. Because it felt so good racing down the mountain with the sun's warmth on my face. The rush of the wind pressing against my cheeks as I plunged down the hill.

I didn't feel out of control. Quite the contrary. I felt like at I was a master of my own destiny. I was freed of the natural constraints that normally bound me. I was moving faster than I could run. I was making more graceful turns I could do if I walking. I was seeing more sights per second than I could possibly take in unless I was driving. It was like magic. I felt like I was in heaven.

I was feeling so elated that I barely noticed the sign as I zipped past it. I had something written in German that I couldn't understand. Why? Because I'd just started my German classes. Because I didn't even take the time to slow down. Because I'd forgotten to bring my German dictionary with me. The one I always kept in my pocket. So, it wouldn't have mattered anyway. Or so I reasoned to myself as I zoomed off the main slope and into the backcountry.

For anyone that's grown up skiing, rule #1 is to know your limits. Know how steep a hill you can ski. Know how fast you can ski. Know what the snow conditions are and ski appropriately. Most importantly, know where you are skiing. And this leads to rule #2. Never ski in the backcountry unless you go with someone else that knows what they are doing. Unless you had prepared for this backcountry. Had avalanche gear on you. and so on.

However, as a young twenty-year-old buck who was having the time of his life, I didn't think about any of these things. None of that was on my mind. No, I was having the time of my life. Skiing fast. Skiing way beyond the groomed trail. I'd found an incredible shoot that I was now skiing down.

Like a surfer riding a huge wave, I skied up and down both sides of the shoot. I'd race up one side of the shoot's wall and then race back down to the center. As soon as I got there, I'd race right up the other side of the shoot. The highest point. Where I felt like I was almost touching the sky. Almost touching the sun. And then zoom! I'd race back down to the shoot's center, and then I'd do it again.

It was a wildly fun time. I felt full of adrenaline. Full of confidence. I was literally brimming with fun inside. I'd forgotten how difficult I was finding it to learn the German language. How languages, unlike math, didn't come so naturally to me. I'd forgotten about the girlfriend who I'd missed terribly ever since I'd left for Germany, and now that I was on this ski hill, at least for this moment in time, she felt like a distant memory.

Swoosh. Zoom. Zip. I went down the backcountry Austrian hill. That seemed to go and go. Like there was no end in sight. I'd never had an experience like it, since in Utah, where I'd grown up skiing, at least at the resorts I frequented, even when you went off trail, it was a few minutes before you reconnected back to main run and made it to the ski lift below.

But that didn't seem to be the case here. It had been over thirty minutes, and I was still skiing down this backcountry hill at full speed, having the time of my life. And then it began to snow. At first softly, and then the snow started to come down harder. I could feel the coolness of the flakes of snow hitting my face. The burning sensation as each snowflake burst when it hit the warmth of my skin.

I liked the sensation and didn't think more about it until the snow started to come down so hard that it began to become harder to see. For the first time in over forty-five minutes, my first worry hit me. The snow was now falling so hard that it was covering my tracks. When I looked behind me, my ski tracks had all been erased by the new snow that was falling fast from the sky. It was like I had become an invisible skier, and on the off chance that this backcountry run didn't reconnect with the ski lift at the bottom, I had a few big problems on my hands.

One, I hadn't told anyone where I was going, so how would they find me, especially because the snow that was rushing down had just erased all my glorious turns? Two, I had no idea where I was. I hadn't taken the time to get a map when I was at the bottom of the ski hill when I'd bought my lift ticket. Not that I was sure that would have helped anyway. Since normally maps show the terrain for the main groomed slopes. Not for the backcountry. And I was in another country. At a resort that I'd never skied before.

I decided wisely that now was not the time to panic. I'd give myself eight hours before I freaked out. Why eight hours? It was the biggest number that popped into my head. It was sixteen times more time than the longest run that I'd ever skied growing up in Utah. Looking back on it, there was no good reason I thought of the number eight hours, but I'm really glad that I did decide that because, boy, what a treacherous next eight hours it would turn out to be.

My amazing ski run ended not at the bottom of the lift but at a stream. I had now spent an hour skiing off trail and had finally reached the point where I could ski no longer. An icy-cold stream cut its way between the steep valley that was on either side of it.

With no place to go and all my ski tracks erased, I had no choice but to take my skis off and try to walk alongside it. However, the banks were too steep, so I finally stopped trying to walk alongside the creek, relented, and walked down the middle of it. The super-cold water burnt and froze my toes. I started to shiver as the warmth in my body confronted water that, if I stayed in it too long, especially as it got deeper and rose up to my waist, I was sure would create hypothermia. While I wasn't trained in such matters, I'd remembered watching a show that discussed how quickly the body could go from its normal temperature to a state where you hit hypothermia and things inside your body didn't go well. Things started to shut down. Your life force was endangered by the power of nature when she wasn't properly respected.

And I hadn't respected her at all. No, I'd been smug. I'd been arrogant. I'd been foolishly brave. And now I way paying the price. I'd walk down the icy-cold stream as long as I could stand it. As long as I could go before I felt like my toes were going to fall off. Then I'd climb out of the water and sit on the side of the creek where in some ways my body felt even colder. Because I wasn't moving. Because I was sitting still. Because the enormity of how dangerous a predicament that I'd put myself in was starting to hit me.

I was in a foreign country. On a foreign slope that I'd never skied before. In the backcountry. Without anyone knowing where I was. Without proper avalanche gear. Without proper, in this case, waterproof gear. I told myself as the panic started to swell to be calm. To trust the universe. To trust in some greater power to help me through this situation.

It was odd that this thought popped in my mind, because I hadn't been raised in a religious family. Quite the opposite. Growing up while everyone else was at church, my stepdad and mom took me to what we called the "Church of the mountains." We spent our Sundays in the outdoors. Skiing. Hiking. Running. Enjoying being out in nature. Not sitting trapped, as we saw it, in a small manmade church. Revering a God that we thought the religious in Utah, Mormonism, had made into a cartoon character. An old wise man with a long white beard. No, our God was the outdoors. Our God was nature.

However, all through growing up and into my teens I'd never thought about God. I'd never thought about a force greater than myself. I'd marveled at how amazing it was, the way the world worked when I'd studied chemistry. Biology. Physics. That the world was an exceedingly complex place. That there was this seamless connection between the molecular level and mountain before me. I hadn't made the connection yet that it was all one and the same, but my analytical mind had loved learning how it was all built. How it all came together.

And now here I was out in the middle of nowhere. Thousands of miles from home. Thousands of miles from my mother. My chemistry classes. My biology classes. My friends. My girlfriend. And I didn't want it to end right here. I didn't want to die of hypothermia or hunger in the middle of an Austrian forest.

I consoled myself that probably I was being a bit overdramatic. That I had to remember that less than an hour ago I'd been having the time of my life. That I'd been in tough situations before and I'd found my way out of them. This would be no different. I would stay calm. I'd stay in the moment. I'd figure it out. I just needed something to grab onto. Something that would help me guide my way.

A simple thought popped into my head. The movement of streams is caused by gravity. That the reason that its molecules tumble one after another is because they are being pulled downhill. And this idea that I was going downhill versus uphill was the first thing my mind could grab onto to give me a bit of hope. Surely if I followed the stream downhill then that would take me to the place at the bottom of the hill where the stream led to something else. Hopefully a city, since I knew from studying European history when I was in high school, that early civilizations formed around rivers. Around streams. Since they were filled with one of the most important things we as humans needed to survive. They were filled with water. I jumped back into the creek and braved its icy waters. I pushed myself to walk down the stream faster. I dropped my skis a couple times and cursed myself out as I had to dive down into the icy waters to retrieve my skis that had sunk to the bottom. The water was unfathomably cold when my head was submerged underwater. I saw stars. For a moment I thought that I was going to faint. And then I popped my head back out of the water and my ears began to ring. They were that cold. I was afraid for a moment that I'd gone deaf since I momentarily couldn't hear anything.

I decided that I was going to leave my skis on the side of the creek. That would make things easier. But then I changed my mind. What if I needed to ski down something steep again? What if that was easier than trying to hike my way down? I'd just gone down a steep shoot of powder that would have been impossible to go down without skis. It was too steep. More importantly, it was probably six-feet-plus deep in powder. Without the skis, which had allowed me to float on top of the fluffy snow, it's likely that I would have sunk down deep and not been able to get out. Not been able to breathe.

I wearily picked up my skis and again began to trudge down the stream. The next two hours were a bit of a blur. The trees that were on both sides of the embankment all looked identical. The water had the same dull brown hue to it now that the sun was starting to go down and its light no longer danced off the water's surface. My legs and feet had gone numb. I was so tired that I wasn't even thinking anymore if I'd done damage to my feet. If they'd need to later get amputated. I was just focused on putting one foot after another.

Finally, I came to a section of the stream where it flattened out. I was elated for a moment because I thought this must mean that I was about to come to a small town. However, I made it around the corner of the now slow-moving stream and there was absolutely nothing there. I'd just spent the last five hours marching down a stream that took me to the base of the valley. I was stuck between two Austrian mountains. And there was no one in sight. Oh boy did I start to feel the panic in me. This was it. I was beyond tired. I felt hungry. Nauseous. Afraid. I couldn't go any farther.

I sat on the side of the embankment. I started to cry. I felt sorry for myself. Angry at myself for doing something so utterly foolish. So dangerous. That I'd put myself in this situation. And then my Inner Voice told me to climb up the side of the muddy embankment to my left. I didn't want to do it, but I couldn't get the thought out of my mind. I couldn't stop thinking about it, so I mustered all my strength and I did it. I put my now interminably heavy skis over my left shoulder and struggled to climb up the muddy, steep slope. It had stopped snowing at this point, and, wherever it was, a bit warmer than where I'd just been before. This had caused some of the snow to melt, and as I climbed higher and higher there were patches of the mountain where there was no snow. Just thick cold mud to climb through. I climbed and climbed for what seemed like an hour. One heavy ski boot covered in mud after the other.

Until I saw it. A tram line. The one thing that told me that things were going to be okay. That if I followed that tram line down. All the way down. It meant that I would get to its terminus. I would get to a ski resort. I would get back to a town. I eagerly put my skis on. It had been six hours. I felt totally frozen inside. I felt beyond tired. However, the thought that things were going to be okay energized me. The thought that I'd listened to my Inner Voice when all hope had seemed lost and now the universe had put out a single item. A single thing that symbolized to me hope. The fact that I had found a tram line that was going to lead me back to safety filled me full of hope.

I started to zoom down the mountain. As fast as I could ski. Unlike where I'd skied before, this side of the mountain faced the sun, and most of the snow by this point had melted away. I skied through mud. I could feel the rocks ripping through the wax on the bottom of my skis. Cutting deep grooves into my fancy skis that I'd rented. But I didn't care. I was beyond thinking about the materiality of things. I had one goal, which was to get back to safety.

And then it happened. A gondola raced above me. A guy yelled down something I couldn't understand in German. Just like with the sign I couldn't understand because it was in a different language, I couldn't understand this man. I didn't stop to yell back and ask him to translate what he'd just said into English because in a flash he was gone. No, I kept racing down the hill and didn't even see it when I skied right off a cliff.

That's what I'd later learn he said in German. He was yelling at me that I was headed straight toward a cliff I'd just skied right off. It was singularly the most terrifying moment of my life. It's the thing you always think cannot happen to you. That you aren't going to be the one who is in the plane that crashes. That you aren't going to be the one who gets hit by the avalanche. That you aren't going to be the one who falls off the side of the mountain. But here it was. I was in that moment where the probability of it happening to me was infinitesimally small. But it had happened. I was free falling at full speed when my ski suit caught a branch that stopped my fall. That saved my life.

I hung upside down, looking at the rocky stream that was right below me. Realizing that in another second, I would have smashed my head against the rock and I would have been dead. Instead, I was tangled up in this tree. My skis had crashed down below me and surprisingly hadn't broken into a million pieces.

After I finally let all of the pure terror release out of me, I untangled myself from the branch, slid the rest of the way down the steep muddy embankment, and fell into the stream until I was neck deep in the water. I'd just had such a scare that I didn't even notice how cold the water was. I was beyond that. I gathered my skis and somehow, I'm still not quite sure how I made it up the other side of the embankment, which wasn't as steep as the one I'd just fallen down. I got to the top and looked down. It was a long, long way down. A brain-bashing distance if I hadn't been saved somehow miraculously by that branch. If the universe, by chance or otherwise, hadn't intervened and broken my fall.

It only took me about another ten minutes to make it down to the bottom of the ski hill. To follow the tram line to its end point. It was now dark outside. I went into the ski bar that was still open. It was my good fortune that Europeans really love to enjoy their post-skiing drink. Their Après-ski.

I must have looked like quite a sight to all the folks who hours ago had stopped skiing and were enjoying a nightcap. I was covered in mud from head to toe. You couldn't even see the red color of my ski suit. My teeth were chattering uncontrollably. I wasn't wearing gloves since they'd frozen stiff long ago. My bare hands were stark white.

I asked in my broken German where I was. One of the bartenders who saw what a mess I was helped me sit down. He told me I was in Germany. I still don't know how I did it, but somehow by the force of my will, my stupidity, and the kindness of the Universe, I'd skied from Austria to Germany.

Flash back to the present. I'm forty-nine years old. I live in Tiburon with my wonderful wife, Christina. My son, Max. I've created a company called Sun Basket that sends out, in my mind, boxes of sunlight. Boxes of goodness. Boxes that are my small attempt to make the world a better place. A healthier place. A more humane place. A place where I want to live in. A place I invite you to live in. I know I still will face huge challenges in my life. I know that it feels like there are more wrong things going on in the world right now than right ones. But I can't control all that. What I can control is how I act. How I feel inside. How I treat other people. How I raise my son, Max. How I fiercely protect my tribe. How I connect with everything around me. How I sound cheesy when I say this, but I don't care. How I become one with the stars, the moon, the sky, the animals, the stream that almost killed me, the ocean where I've almost died surfing, and everything that's all around me. I've found my connection to the Universe. I've made my peace with it. I've found my eternal sunshine. I invite you to join me.

Acknowledgments

I would like to take a moment to thank all the people that made this book possible. First and foremost to my wonderful wife Christina who puts up with me, and reminds me every day about the importance of balancing work and family. I'd also like to thank my son, Max, who is the funniest person I know. At twenty months, he makes me laugh and see the brighter side of life more every day. His enthusiasm for life is infectious! While I relate some hard times I had with my parents, I am forever grateful to them. My mom, Michelle, is one of the most intuitive people and a trailblazer in her own way as a psychologist, mom, and former intrepid mountain climber. She taught me the importance, when we were fly-fishing, of always making sure you had one foot firmly planted in a fast rushing stream before you took another step forward. My father, Bert, is one of the humblest and kindest people I know, despite being one of the most successful cancer researchers of his generation—he discovered 4 of the first 20 genes that cause hereditary cancer. He taught me that hard work, tenacity, and learning to focus on problems that can be solved can create tremendous success and personal fulfillment. My stepfather, Mike, raised me with my mom. I will be forever grateful for his life lessons that include: comparisons are odious and the importance of the golden rule. One of the most joyous men that I've ever met, who switched from working as a think tank economist to becoming a modern dancer and teacher, Mike taught me the importance of following my dreams. And to my stepmom, Suzi. She took me to my first cooking classes, which inspired my lifelong love of cooking and great food.

While my family continues to me be my "inner tribe," I am indebted to a small group of guys who became my lifelong friends. Tom, Matt, Praveen, Rom, Braxton, and Tyler are my best buds for life. Without them, my struggles in my twenties and early thirties would not have been nearly as fun! While I relate some tough times that we went through together as I sought to live a healthier life, I'm forever grateful for their unwavering friendship—especially since they are the keepers of all sorts of embarrassing stories about me. On the work side, my grandfather George remains my entrepreneur hero. As the co-founder of TCI, which became Liberty Media, George was a quiet visionary who not only created products of the future, but cared deeply about their impact on the community. He sold his cable assets so he could focus on his local media companies, particularly local news, which he viewed as vital to our democracy. My entrepreneurial journey would never have started without partnering first with Braxton, one of the most brilliant technologists of his generation, who created the first large-scale mobile media networks. Together, we built one of the first mobile social networks, which won a Webby and was ahead of its time. It was a real-time social analytics platform used by over 500 large enterprise firms, and the platform for the healthy eating platform that Sun Basket has become. I'm deeply thankful for Steve and Chad, the founders of YouTube, believing in Braxton and me and buying our former company. While things didn't work out, I will forever hold Chad and Steve in the highest regard as some of the most amazing entrepreneurs in Silicon Valley who created one of my favorite sites: YouTube. And the team at Sun Basket. What can I say? Over 1,700 people work incredibly hard every day delivering millions of healthy meals nationwide each month. They make me look good. They make me proud. None of it would be possible without my incredible executive team which all started with our incomparably talented Chef Justine and my glorious co-founders George, Tyler, and Don. They are all truly unique and special human beings that help me re-learn the lesson every day that can do good by doing good. While sometimes I ask the moon and the stars why I raised venture capital since investors, when things aren't going well can be really tough on you, I'm blessed to have backers who are incredibly good human beings and great business minds. My thanks go out to the first investors who believed in Sun Basket—Tim and Steve—as well as Albert, my first and forever most favorite banker. I'm also thankful for Judy who served as a second mother to me, gave me my first job after working at McKinsey & Company to support my artistic and entrepreneurial dreams. I'm thankful to Ian who's an even worse surfer than me, despite the fact he'll forever claim otherwise. Big shout to Chris, a fellow entrepreneur who is just as crazy as I am. And finally a thanks to the French interviewer who called me a failsafe entrepreneur. He made me work doubly hard to prove him wrong. To prove to him that through inspiration, determination, and following my intuition I could realize my dreams. One step at a time. Into the sunlight. Not forgetting the past. But leaving it behind.

About the Author

Adam Zbar is a Webby-winning serial entrepreneur. He is the CEO and founder of Sun Basket, the leading healthy personal eating platform in the US. The company's mission is that Food Is Medicine. In just 4 years since launch, the company has experienced tremendous growth going from $0–300M and 0–1700 employees by solving American's #1 food need: What's for dinner? In a delicious, easy way that's personalized for your healthy lifestyle. Zbar is the genetic misfit son of a successful. analytical cancer scientist and a mercurial, highly intuitive psychologist mother. His entire life he's struggled between balancing his left-brain analytic self with his right-brain creative self. In *Shine*, Adam tells of his journey from hitting rock bottom at the age of 39 when he was 50 pounds overweight, getting a divorce, and his start-up was failing, to finally listening to his inner voice and rebuilding his life from the inside out. To losing 50 pounds in three months and in the process creating what has become one of America's fastest growing healthy food companies that is disrupting the $1T food system with the vision that Food Is Medicine.

Zbar lives in Tiburon, California with his wonderful wife, Christina, his son, Max, and their dog, Barbara. He wrote this book with one purpose: To help inspire you—as he did—to become your best self. To lose weight you always wanted to. To follow your dreams and create the business or other project you wanted to do. To literally start to shine from the inside out.

CPSIA information can be obtained
at www.ICGtesting.com
Printed in the USA
LVHW070951190319
611138LV00014B/118/P